MW00987463

ST. PATRICK

His Confession
and Other Works

St. Patrick
Bishop and Apostle of Ireland

ST. PATRICK
His Confession and Other Works

TRANSLATION BY
FR. NEIL XAVIER O'DONOGHUE

CATHOLIC BOOK PUBLISHING CORP.
NEW JERSEY

NIHIL OBSTAT: Rev. C. Anthony Ziccardi, S.T.D. S.S.L.
Censor Librorum

IMPRIMATUR: ✠ Most Rev. John J. Myers, D.D., J.C.D.
Archbishop of Newark

Homily of Pope John Paul II on His Pastoral Visit to Drogheda, Co. Louth, 1979 used with permission. © Libreria Editrice Vaticana.

Texts of the Mass of St. Patrick are provided for devotional use courtesy of the National Centre for Liturgy, St Patrick's College, Maynooth, Co. Kildare, Ireland.

The Scripture quotations contained in the Novena are from the New Revised Standard Version Bible: Catholic Edition copyright © 1993 and 1989 by the Division of Christian Education of the National Council of Churches of Christ in the U.S.A. Used by permission. All rights reserved.

Cover Icon of St. Patrick in the paperback edition © Transfiguration Monastery, Brookline, MA, used with permission.

(T-178)

ISBN 978-0-89942-179-7 (paperback)
ISBN 978-0-89942-181-0 (hardcover)

© 2009 Catholic Book Publishing Corp., N.J.

Printed in Korea
wwwcatholicbookpublishing.com

CONTENTS

FOREWORD

MOST people know of some of the popular traditions associated with St. Patrick such as the casting out of all snakes from Ireland or the use of the shamrock as a symbol of the Trinity. However relatively few have ever read the Saint's two surviving works translated in this small book. It is our hope that by reading the *Confessio* and the *Letter to Coroticus and His Soldiers* (which modern historians unanimously accept as having come from the pen of St. Patrick himself) many more people can get to meet St. Patrick the man and discover his relevance for the twenty-first century.

The texts have been translated with the aim of letting St. Patrick speak for himself, without encumbering them with many notes or entering into discussions that are only of interest to specialists.[1] A number of other sections have been added to this work to help us meet St. Patrick. *The Life of St. Patrick* is taken from the 1911 edition of the *Catholic Encyclopedia* and provides a fuller historical picture drawing on later historical documents and traditions. Likewise the beautiful discourse of Pope John Paul II from his pastoral visit to Drogheda (within the archdiocesan boundaries of Armagh whose bishop is the successor of St. Patrick and Primate of All Ireland) is a very moving reminder from the succes-

---

[1] I have translated from the Latin original as found in David R. Howlett, *The Book of Letters of Saint Patrick the Bishop* (Dublin: Four Courts Press, 1994). Those interested in continuing to study St. Patrick and his world are advised to consult the Further Reading list at the end of this book.

sor of Peter of the continued relevance of Ireland's Apostle. Finally this book ends with a newly composed Novena to St. Patrick based on early Irish sources and the official Mass of St. Patrick for personal prayer.

It is our hope that this little book will help foster devotion to St. Patrick anew and help yet another generation of Christians to join their lives to Christ in prayer as St. Patrick himself did so many years ago as a slave herding sheep on the barren mountain of Slemish.

Fr. Neil Xavier O'Donoghue
Kearny, New Jersey
Feast of St. Brigid, Abbess,
Secondary Patron of Ireland
February 1, 2009

1

The *Confessio* or Confession of St. Patrick

The Confessio *of St. Patrick cannot be considered an autobiography in the modern sense. While it would be nice to have a modern autobiography of Ireland's national Saint, the* Confessio *is, perhaps, a still more important document. Although it may not contain as many details about St. Patrick's life as we would like, it gives us a window into his soul. What matters for us today is not so much that we might identify the exact location of Bannauenta Berniae or the wood of Voclut. What truly matters, and what the* Confessio *offers to us, is the possibility to partake of the same divine life that St. Patrick brought to Ireland.*

St. Patrick's world of the fifth century in Western Europe was an adventurous time coming between the Roman Empire and the birth of the Middle Ages. As the old order of the Empire passed away a new Europe was born. The unity of this new Europe was to be based on a common Christian heritage. As missionaries embarked on their apostolic expeditions, new lands were incorporated into this new Christendom. Ireland was in fact the first new region to be evangelized outside the frontiers of the Roman Empire and so brought into the fold of Chris-

tendom. The **Confessio** *provides a fascinating firsthand account of the evangelization of Ireland written by the man who subsequent generations of Irish people would unanimously recognize as their patron saint.*

It seems that St. Patrick wrote the **Confessio** *in order to defend himself against accusations made against him in his native Britain. He was probably an old man approaching his final days and unable to travel back to Britain in person (for reasons of age, and because of the needs of his mission). Therefore he introduces the reader to the circumstances that led him to Ireland in the first place as a slave and to his return later on as a missionary bishop. He also takes time to explain some details of the mission itself. As we hear nothing else about the accusations laid against him, it is probable that they came to nothing. However they did have the beneficial consequence of forcing St. Patrick to write this important document.*

(1) I Patrick, am a sinner, the most uncultured and smallest among all the faithful, indeed many people consider me to be worthless.[1] I am the son of the deacon Calpornius, and grandson of the priest Potitus.[2] My father was from the village of Ban-

---

[1] While St. Patrick's protestations of his own poverty are to be admired for their humility, a number of recent studies have shown that he was in fact quite cultured and, while not as educated as a professional scholar, he was well able to write in the Latin of the day respecting the conventions of oratory and style.

[2] In the early Church it was not unknown for mature married men to be ordained as priests; usually after their Ordination these men and their wives would assume a life of chastity.

nauenta Berniae, he had a villa nearby.[3] It was there that I was captured when I was almost sixteen years old. I did not really know the true God when I was brought in slavery to Ireland together with thousands of others. All of us deserved this slavery because *we had turned away from God,* and *did not keep His commandments.*[4] We had not been obedient to our priests, who were encouraging us to do those things necessary for salvation. God *brought his anger down upon us and scattered us among many nations* indeed *even to the ends of the earth.*[5] It is here that I now find myself, small as I am, among strangers. (2) Here *the Lord revealed to me my sense of unbelief* so that I could repent of my sins and *turn with my whole heart to the Lord my God.* God *looked at my misery* and had mercy upon my youth and ignorance. He watched over me before I knew Him and before I could tell right from wrong: He had compassion for me just as a father has for his son.

---

[3] Despite many theories, in reality we have no idea where this town was. All that can be said with certainty is that it was somewhere on the current island of Great Britain (see chapter 23), possibly on the north-western coast as this would have been accessible to Irish pirates. Ethnically St. Patrick belonged to the descendants of the Roman-British colony. The question of his being English is nonsensical given that the Anglo-Saxon tribes which were to form the cultural nucleus of the English people hadn't yet invaded Britain.

[4] St. Patrick often quotes from Scripture in his writings. In this translation these quotations are marked by italics, but in the interest of simplicity each Biblical citation is not identified, for information on specific quotations the reader is directed to one of the scholarly editions of the Saint's writings.

[5] The knowledge that with his mission Christianity had reached the end of the earth (at least in the early Medieval world) was of great significance to St. Patrick and it adds to his understanding of the importance of his own place in the history of the Church. The evangelization of Ireland was also the first time that Christianity traveled outside the borders of the former (Western) Roman Empire.

(3) I cannot be silent, *nor would it be helpful,* about all the gifts and graces that the Lord in His mercy bestowed upon me in *the land of my slavery.* Indeed this is how we ought to behave. After being punished by God we must *praise Him and tell of His marvels to every nation under the heavens.*

(4) Because there is no other God, nor was there any before Him nor will there be after Him. For He is God the Father unbegotten and ungenerated, who is the source of every beginning and, as we have learned, holds all things in being. We declare that His Son Jesus Christ has always been with the Father. Before time began He was spiritually begotten by the Father in an inexplicable way. Through Christ all things visible and invisible were made. He was made man, He overcame death, He was received into Heaven by the Father *who gave Him all sovereignty over every name in Heaven, on the earth and under the earth, that every tongue should confess His name. For Jesus Christ is Lord and God,* in whom we believe and whose coming we await in the near future. He will be *Judge of the living and the dead, who will reward every man as his deeds deserve* and *who will pour out an abundance of the Holy Spirit upon us as the gift* and *pledge* of immortality. This Holy Spirit makes believers and those who obey God into *children of God* and *coheirs of Christ* as we confess and adore the one God in the Trinity of holy Names.

(5) He Himself has said through the prophet: *Call on me in the day of your tribulation and I will free you and you will proclaim my greatness.* And again he says *how good it is to proclaim and confess the works of God.* (6) Even though I am imperfect in so many ways, I want *my brothers and friends* to know my true

feelings so that they can appreciate the true desire of my soul. (7) I do not ignore *my Lord's witness* which testifies in the psalms that *those who tell lies will be lost.* And again says *the lying mouth kills the soul.* The same Lord has said in the Gospel, *on the day of judgment men will have to give an explanation for every idle word which they have spoken.* (8) Therefore, I ought to worry exceedingly *with fear and trembling* the sentence of that day when none can escape or hide and all will have *to give an account* even of the smallest of sins *before the judgment seat of Christ the Lord.*

(9) Therefore, although I have long wished to write, I hesitated *until the present time* as I feared the *murmuring of the tongues of men.* Unlike the others I did not study law and the sacred sciences in an excellent balance. These men, unlike me, were not obliged to change their language in their youth, but were able to perfect their native tongue.[6] However, my own *words and speech* had to be translated into a strange language and I had very little training and formal education. This can be easily seen from the quality of my writing; as Scripture says, *the wise man will be known by his speech and by his insight and perception and true doctrine.* (10) But of what use is an excuse, even if it is *true,* if it is given with the presumption of one who tries to accomplish in old age that which he neglected *in his youth*? My sins did not allow me to fully learn what I had briefly studied. But who would believe me even if I were to say everything again?

---

[6] This suggestion that Latin was his native tongue (although, unlike his contemporaries, his schooling was interrupted by his slavery in Ireland) is another indication of St. Patrick's Roman-British heritage.

I was made a slave as a teenager, at an age when I could hardly speak and before I knew what I should do and what I should avoid. Even today I blush and am very embarrassed by my lack of learning. I am quite unable to express my story in the same way as those people who are well trained in the art of precise writing, and my words do not express exactly that which my spirit feels. (11) If I had received as many talents as the others, I would be quick to speak aloud and say that which needs to be said. However, if it seems to some that I am too presumptuous for speaking anyway in my hesitant and *slow speech,* it must be remembered that Scripture says *the tongues of stammers quickly learn to speak words of peace.* How much more must we strive to do this because we are *a letter written by Christ for the salvation even of the remotest parts of the earth.* Although this letter may not be refined it is very strong and true, *written in your hearts not with ink but with the spirit of the living God.* And again the Spirit bears witness that *even the plainest things have been created by the Most High.*

(12) Above all else I am a simple man, an unlearned refugee who *does not know how to provide for the future.* But *I know for definite* that *before I was humbled* I was like a stone lying *in the deep mud.* But *the Strong One* came and *in His mercy* He took me out and He lifted me on high and placed me on the top of His wall. Therefore, I must cry aloud *in thanksgiving* to *the Lord* for so many good things which He has given me both now and for eternity, things so great that the mind of man can never grasp.

(13) Be filled with awe *all you men small and great who fear God* and you lords and teachers listen and

examine this. Who is it who took me in my ignorance and raised me above those whom you know to
be wise and experts in the law and *powerful in speech*
and every talent? I who am detestable to this world,
have been inspired above these others. He did this
for me on behalf of the people to whom the *love of
Christ* had taken me. So that *with fear and reverence*
and *without blame,* if I am found worthy, I might
spend my life humbly serving them.

(14) It is through the power of our faith in the
Trinity that I decided to write without fear, even
though there are many dangers, so that many can
know the *gift of God* and His *eternal consolation* and so
that the knowledge of the Name of God, Who is ever
faithful, can be spread far and wide. This will also
mean *that after my life is over* I can leave an inheritance
for my brothers and sisters, those thousands of my
children whom I have Baptized into the Lord. (15) I
am not worthy of all this. But the Lord has had mercy
on this pitiable slave and after so many calamities and
disasters and after many years of slavery among these
people, He has given me so many more graces than I
could even have imagined in my youth.

(16) When I came to Ireland I spent each day
tending sheep and I prayed many times during the
day.[7] Thus I grew more and more in the love of God.
And as the fear of God increased in me so did my
faith, so that in a single day I would pray up to one
hundred times and in the course of the night I would

---

[7] This experience of the consolation of prayer was fundamental for
the strengthening of St. Patrick's Christian faith. Irish Christianity
was born from the prayers of this British slave who had been sent as
a shepherd in the midst of many hardships. Seventh century tradition
identifies the mountain of Slemish, Co. Antrim as the place where St.
Patrick tended sheep.

pray nearly as many times again. When I was tending
the sheep on mountains and in woods and in the
dark before the dawn I would awaken and pray in the
snow, in the frost and in the rain. No harm came to
me as there was no idleness in me, as I can now see,
for my spirit was always fervent.

(17) It was there that one night I heard a voice in
my sleep saying to me, "How good it is that you are
fasting, you will soon return to your own country." A
little while later I heard the voice again, it said,
"Behold, your ship is ready." But the ship was a long
way off, about two hundred miles and I had never
been in that place nor did I know anybody there. So
shortly after this I ran away and left the man to
whom I had been enslaved for the past six years. By
the strength of God, Who has always guided me in
good places, I fearlessly reached the ship.

(18) The day I arrived the ship was about to set
sail. I spoke with them saying that I could pay my passage, but the captain got angry with me and retorted,
"You shall not come with us." Hearing this I made my
way back to the little cabin where I was taking refuge.
As I walked I prayed and before my prayer was finished I heard one of the sailors shout after me, "Come
quickly for these men are calling you." I ran back to
them and they said to me, "Hurry up, we'll take you
on faith, become our friend in whatever way you think
best." However that day I would not suck their breasts
out of fear of God, but I hoped that they would come
to faith in Jesus Christ for they were pagans.[8] Thus, I
fell in with them and we set sail at once.

---

[8] It is not very clear what St. Patrick means here, but he may well
be referring to ancient Irish pagan religious rites or traditional
demonstrations of friendship.

(19) Three days later we landed, but for twenty-eight days we made our way through a deserted country.[9] Our food ran out and *hunger overpowered* the crew. The captain came to me and said, "Why has this happened, Christian? You say that your God is great and all-powerful, why then are you not praying for us? We could easily starve to death and may never see anyone else again." Full of confidence I said to him, "Convert and turn with your whole heart to the Lord my God, for nothing is impossible to Him. If you do this, today He will send you food enough for the journey for He owns an abundance everywhere."

By the help of God it came to pass: behold in front of our very eyes a herd of pigs appeared on the roadway. The crew was able to kill a lot of them. We stayed there for two days and ate a lot of pork and recovered our strength, for many of them were weak and half-dead with hunger. Then they gave great thanks to God and I also was held in high esteem by them. From that day on they had food in abundance. They even found some wild honey, they offered me some, but thank God, I did not taste it, for one of them later told me that they had offered it in sacrifice.[10]

---

[9] This "deserted country" may refer to the desperate situation of Britain after the Roman Legions had withdrawn and the province gradually disintegrated.

[10] Obviously the ancient Irish, like many other pagan peoples, practiced the custom of offering food to the pagan deities. No self-respecting Christian could afterwards partake of these foods. While it might seem far from us today it was a major issue in the early Church. St. Paul deals with this problem in 1 Corinthians 8. Here he says that while there is no objective problem for a Christian to eat these foods, that they ought to abstain from them so as not to scandalize those whose faith is weak. In the ancient world this would often make it impossible for Christians to eat meat as most commercially available meat had been sacrificed to idols before it made it to the marketplace.

(20) That same night as I was asleep Satan tempted me. This temptation was stronger than I ever experienced and I will remember it as long as I am *in this body.* He fell on me like a huge stone and I couldn't move any part of my body. I don't know how it happened, but in my ignorance I thought to call upon Elijah.[11] I saw that the sun was rising in the sky and while I started calling out at the top of my voice, "Elijah! Elijah!" behold the splendor of the sun fell upon me and immediately all the weight left me. I believe that it was Christ Jesus who came to my aid and His Spirit went so far as to cry out on my behalf. I hope that this is what it will be like *on the day of* my *testing,* as the Lord says in the Gospel, *on that day it will not be you who speak, but the Spirit of my Father will speak on your behalf.*

(21) Once again many years later I was taken captive again. The first night that I was with my captors, I received a divine message that said to me "You will only be with them for two months." It happened exactly like this: on the sixtieth night *the Lord rescued me from their hands.* (22) Besides the food, the Lord granted us dry weather and fire for the rest of the journey, these lasted for ten days until we met some people. As I said above, we had been journeying for twenty-eight days altogether and the day we came upon other people was the very day our food ran out.

(23) Once again, I spent a few short years with my family in Britain. They welcomed me back as a son and begged that because of the hardships I had suffered I should never leave them again. But it hap-

---

[11] This Old Testament Saint has always been a favorite in monastic circles. Perhaps this is indicative of the important role monasticism was later to play in the Irish Church.

pened that there *one night as if in a vision* I saw a man come from Ireland. His name was Victor and it was as if he was bringing thousands of letters to me. He gave me one of them and I read the first line which started "The voice of the Irish." As I started to read it was as if I could hear the voices of the people who were living at the wood of Voclut which is near the Western Sea.[12] These shouted out *as if in one voice:* "We implore you, O holy boy, to come here and be with us." My *heart was rent within me* and I could read no further and I woke up. Thanks be to God that he listened to their cry after so many years. (24) On another night, either in me or besides me (I do not know which *but the Lord knows*) I heard very learned words, and I could understand none of them except the very last ones which said "The One Who gave His life for you, He it is Who is speaking to you." Then I awoke full of joy.

(25) Another time I saw someone praying as if it were inside me or with me inside the depths of my being and I could hear Him above me, or above the *interior man.* He was praying very strongly with groans. I was greatly surprised and wondered who it could be that was praying in me. But at the end of the prayer He told me that he was the Spirit. I had experienced what I remembered the Apostle saying that "the Spirit helps us in the weakness of our prayer. For we do not know how we ought to pray, but the Spirit Himself intercedes on our behalf with groanings that cannot be put into words."

(26) When I was tested by some of my elders who came to me and said that I was not fit to fulfill

---

[12] Since the seventh century this has been identified as the wood near Killala, Co. Mayo.

a bishop's ministry because of my sins, I was so strongly *overcome that I nearly fell* for all eternity. But the Lord looked kindly on this exile and pilgrim for His Name's sake and He helped me greatly in this trial. Despite their words and my shame I suffered no harm—may the Lord *not hold this sin against them.* (27) They discovered this charge against me thirty years after it had happened.[13]

I had confessed it before being ordained a deacon. In my anxiety I had told this sin to my dearest friend, a sin I had committed one day, indeed it lasted less than an hour, and this had happened in that time when I still followed my evil inclinations. *God knows* but I think I was not yet fifteen years old. I had not as yet come to believe in the living God, but from my infancy I remained in death and unbelief until I was truly punished *and in true humility suffered hunger and nakedness* for many days. (28) Indeed I did not get to go to Ireland until these humiliations had nearly killed me. But this was providential for by this I was purified by the Lord. He thus prepared me to be the kind of person I am today so that I can care and work for the salvation of others; me who never cared for my own salvation.

(29) On the very night following this day of my humiliation by those mentioned above I had anoth-

---

[13] There is no way of knowing what this sin was which St. Patrick committed as a teenager before being enslaved in Ireland (we only know that whatever it was it lasted less than an hour and happened only once). He revealed it to his friend and spiritual director before he was ordained, probably as part of spiritual direction and not within the Sacrament of Confession. This man may well have been the Metropolitan or Archbishop who entrusted him with the Irish mission (see Chapter 32). Initially this friend saw no problem, but decades later at the time that the *Confessio* was composed he had changed his mind and now was persecuting St. Patrick for this past sin.

er vision. Before my face there appeared a writing that dishonored me, but I heard the voice of God which said to me "We have seen the face of our chosen one deprived of his honor." He did not say "you have seen" but "we have seen" as if He were including Himself. As He says, "whoever touches you it is as if he is touching the apple of My eye."

(30) *I give thanks to the One who strengthens me* in all things. He has not hindered me in the course of action I was taking or that mission that Christ Jesus had shown me. I felt a great strength from Him so that my good faith was approved in the sight of God and men. (31) I can boldly say that my conscience neither reproved me then nor in the future. As God is my witness I have told no lies to you in this account.

(32) My only sorrow is for my dear friend, for thanks to him we have had to hear such a report. I had entrusted my very soul to him. Some brothers told me before this trial (which I had not petitioned for, nor was I even in Britain when it took place) that in my absence he was going to stand for me. Indeed it was from his very lips that I had heard "Look you are going to be raised to the rank of bishop" even though he knew then that I was unworthy. How strange it is that later on, whether it be for good or bad, that he would publicly dishonor me in a thing that he had earlier given me, and not he alone, but the Lord also granted that I become a bishop.[14]

---

[14] Perhaps the hardest part of this persecution that St. Patrick had to bear was that the ringleader used to be his best friend and that it seems that this man who had arranged for St. Patrick to become a bishop (even though he already knew of the past sin) was now trying to arrange for him to be stripped of his office on the basis of this childhood transgression.

(33) I have said enough, even though I must not hide *the gift of God* that was generously bestowed on me *in the land of my captivity.* I looked hard for Him then and I found Him. I believe that He saved me from all iniquity *because of the indwelling of* His *Spirit,* which has been active in me since that day. I speak boldly. But God knows that I do so because it was He Himself who revealed this to me and that if these things had been revealed to me by a mere man I would have held my tongue for *the love of Christ.*

(34) I give constant thanks to God Who has kept me faithful *in the day of my trial.* To this day I offer my soul to Him *as a living sacrifice* to Christ the Lord, for He has *saved me from all my anguish.* I can truly ask, who am I, O Lord? And why have You called me? Why have You poured out so many divine graces upon me, so that today I can *exalt and magnify Your name among the pagans* in whatever place I find myself? Indeed not only when things are well, but also when they go badly, so that in evil or good, I always raise up thanks to God Who has shown me that I must never doubt Him. He has inspired me *in these last days* to start this fundamental and marvelous work. In this way I imitate those of whom the Lord once prophesied would announce His gospel *as a witness to all nations* until *the end of the world.* Behold, it is just as we foresaw, for we are witnesses that the Gospel has been preached in this place beyond which no one else lives.[15]

(35) It would be too long for me to tell the whole story of all my labors or even just to tell some parts of it. Suffice it to say the Lord rescued me from slavery

---

[15] Again St. Patrick bears witness to the ancient understanding of geography which considered the world to end in the waters beyond Ireland and therefore with his mission Christianity had reached the ends of the earth.

many times and saved my life from mortal danger twelve times over—not to mention the many plots against me *which I am not able to express in words.* I don't want to make my readers too bored, but as God is my witness (and He knows all things before they come to pass), He often gave me, poor wretch that I am, divine messages forewarning me of future dangers. (36) *How did I come by this wisdom?* Surely it was not my own for I neither knew *the number of my days* nor who God was. How come I was later to be given such a great gift of knowing and loving God even if this meant leaving my home and family?

(37) So many gifts were offered to me with sorrow and tears. I offended some of the donors and my seniors against my will. With God as my guide I did not give in to them or agree with them in any way. This is not of my own doing but rather it is the work of God, Who lives in me and overcomes all of my problems. When I came to preach the Gospel to the Irish pagans and to suffer abuse at the hands of unbelievers, *I heard strong criticism of my pilgrimage* and bore many persecutions *even to the point of being bound in chains* and I gave up my birthright of freedom for the sake of others.

Indeed if I am judged worthy, I am more than ready to *freely* give *my very life* for the sake of His name. I want to *pour out* my life here *until I die,* if God be willing. (38) For I am most truly in God's debt. He has given me so many graces, so many people have been reborn for eternal life in God and afterwards confirmed and some have been ordained as clergy throughout this land, for these people who are just coming to the Faith. These people God has taken *from the ends of the earth,* as He once promised in the

Prophets, *People shall come to you from the ends of the earth and they shall say to you, "Our fathers falsely worshiped useless idols."* And God also prophesied, *I have set you as a light for the pagans so that you may be salvation for the ends of the earth.*

(39) I wish to wait there for the promise of Him Who never goes back on His word as is said in the Gospel: "They will come from east and west and recline with Abraham, and Isaac, and Jacob." Thus we believe that believers will come from every part of the world. (40) Therefore we ought to fish well in accordance with what the Lord says: *Follow me and I will make you fishers of men.* And as He says in the Prophets, *Thus says the Lord, behold I send out many fishermen and hunters,* etc. Therefore it is good for us to cast our net, so that *a great and vast multitude* may be caught by God and that everywhere there may be clergy to baptize and exhort people who are in need and searching. This is just what the Lord says, and teaches, and advises in the Gospel, *Go therefore and teach all peoples, baptizing them in the name of the Father and of the Son and of the Holy Spirit, teaching them to observe everything I have told you. Behold I will be with you always even until the end of the ages.* Again He says, *Go into the whole world, preach the Gospel to every creature; whoever believes and is baptized will be saved, whoever does not will be condemned.*

And yet again He says, *Preach this Gospel of the Kingdom throughout the world as a witness to all peoples and then the end will come.* This is also what the Lord foretold through the Prophets, *During the last days, says the Lord, I will pour out my Spirit on all flesh, and your sons and daughters will prophesy and your young men will see visions and your old men will dream dreams and upon my slaves and maidservants I will pour out my Spirit on those days and they will prophesy.* In Hosea he says, *I will rename "no-people-of-mine" "my-people" and "she-who-has-not-been-shown-mercy" shall also be renamed "she-who-has-been-shown-mercy." In the same place that I told you "you are not my sons" you will be called "sons of the living God."*

(41) How come that in Ireland where there was no knowledge of God and idols and unclean things were worshiped *now they have become a people of God* and sons of God? How come the sons and daughters of Irish kings are becoming monks and virgins consecrated to Christ? (42) One particular Irish woman, who was both noble and beautiful and whom I had baptized, came to me a few days afterwards and told me that she had received a message from God to become a virgin of Christ and to draw close to God. Thank God she accomplished this six days later in a most excellent way.

In a like manner so do all the virgins, even if their parents are not in agreement. Although they undergo persecutions and false accusations from their families, their numbers still increase, indeed the number of these women who were reborn into our fellowship is beyond counting, not to mention the many widows and others living in continence. The ones that work hardest are those women who are in slavery; they are constantly in danger and being threatened. But God has given this grace to many of his maidservants, and although they are forbidden they follow Him all the more strongly.[16]

---

[16] It would seem that St. Patrick himself established some early form of monasticism in his Irish mission. It is interesting to note that the abundance of vocations is perhaps the greatest sign to St. Patrick that his mission has been blessed by God.

(43) How could I, even if I do desire it, leave them and go to Britain? I would love to visit my home and family, and not only there, but also to go to Gaul and visit the brethren there and to see the faces of the holy ones of my God.[17] God knows that I dearly desire this, but *I am tied by the Spirit* Who *protests* to me that He would *bear witness against me* if I were to do this. He would hold me responsible in the future if I did this and I am afraid of undoing the work that I have started. It is not I but Christ the Lord who ordered me to come to these people and to stay with them for the rest of my life. *If it be the will of God* He will keep my feet from evil ways so that I do not *sin against them.*

(44) This is my hope and my duty, although I do not trust myself a*s long as I am in this body destined to death.* But I am faced with a strong enemy who every day tempts me against true faith and chaste religion. But I have committed the rest of my life to Christ my Lord. But *the flesh is an enemy* that always betrays us to death, that tempts me to the satisfaction of evil desires. I have some insight into this because I have not lived as perfect a life as other believers, but I still trust in my Lord. I do not blush before God for I have not lied. Indeed *from my youth* when I came to know the love of God and to fear Him *until this day* I have been the Lord's *faithful servant.*

(45) Whoever wishes can laugh at me and insult me. I will not be silent nor shall I hide the signs and

---

[17] Various traditions about St. Patrick point to his links to Gaul (modern-day France)and the Christianity and monasticism of this local Church. He may have received his clerical training in a monastery in Gaul.

wonders that the Lord has shown me; signs He has
shown me years before they happened, as is proper
for Him Who knows everything *even before time
began.* (46) Therefore I give unending praise to
God. He has often forgiven my folly, my negligence
and more than once He has spared me from His
anger. Even if I was called to be His helper, I was not
very quick to do what was revealed to me according
to *the suggestion of the Spirit.*

The Lord *had mercy on me a million times* for He
saw what His *plan* was for me, even if I myself did
not know how to act due to the many people who
were hindering me. They used even to talk about me
behind my back and say, "Why does this fellow want
to place himself in danger among the crowds of people who do not know God?" It was not out of malice that they did this, but as I myself bear witness,
they did not think my mission was a good idea due
to my lack of education. I did not understand the
grace that this persecution was for me at the time,
but I understand it now.

(47) Now I have given a simple account to my
brothers and fellow workers. These have believed in
me because *I preached and still preach* to strengthen
and confirm your faith. I wish you also would strive
to do bigger and better things. This would be my
glory for *the wise son is his father's glory.*

(48) You know, as God also knows, how I behaved
in your midst *from my youth* in true faith *and sincerity
of heart.* Even among the pagans with whom I lived, I
have kept and still keep the faith. God knows I have
defrauded none of them for the sake of God and His
Church. The thought of this never crossed my mind,
lest they persecute or blaspheme the name of God. As

Scripture says, "Alas for the man who causes the Lord's name to be blasphemed."

(49) Even though *I am unskilled in all things* I still tried not to accept anything from the Christian brethren or the virgins of Christ or pious women who tried to give me gifts without my asking for them. They laid gifts on the altar from their jewelry and were shocked at me when I returned these to them. But I was looking towards that eternal hope, and I was careful in all my affairs, so that no one could find me unfaithful nor could they find me ministering for the sake of earthly gain. I gave no opportunity for unbelievers to speak badly or criticize me. (50) Did I charge as much as a penny to any of the thousands I baptized? *Tell me and I will return it.* Or when, in my littleness, the Lord allowed me to ordain many clerics, did I take advantage to ask even one of them for as much as the price of a shoe? If this be true *tell me and I will repay you* many times over.[18]

(51) Actually, *I spent* money on your behalf so that you *might accept* me. I traveled among you and to many other places as a pilgrim experiencing many dangers. I went to the most outlying parts, beyond which no one lives, and there where no one had ever done so before I baptized and confirmed people and ordained clergy. It was through the grace of God that I freely and generously did all these things on your behalf. (52) All along I gave presents to kings and paid the expenses of their sons who traveled with me. They even abducted me and my companions and

---

[18] St. Patrick established a full Church in Ireland with its own clergy. He was also very careful to avoid the sin of simony (charging a price for the celebration of the Sacraments) which was to be a problem throughout the medieval period.

one day they even tried to kill me, even though my
time had not come. They stole everything that we
had with us and bound me in irons. But on the four-
teenth day the Lord freed me from their power and
they returned everything to us by the power of God
and thanks to some *providential friends* whom we had
had the fortune to know beforehand.

(53) You yourselves have also had the experience
of how much I paid the judges *in all the regions* that
I frequently visited.[19] I think that I must have paid
them at least the price of fifteen slaves, so that you
could be with me and so that I could always be with
you in the Lord. I am not sorry for this, indeed I will
continue paying these fees. God is powerful and
afterward He will grant that *I may spend my very self
on your behalf.*

(54) Behold, *I call upon God as my witness that I
am not lying.* I do not write to you out of flattery or
avarice, nor am I hoping for honor from you. For me
it is enough to have that honor that no eye sees but
which the heart believes in. *The One who makes the
promise is faithful and does not lie.* (55) For I realize
that *in this present age* I have been raised up by the
Lord above all measure. I am neither worthy nor
even a good choice for all this. I know for certain
that I am better suited for poverty and calamity than
for riches and delights. But *Christ Jesus became poor*
for us and I myself am lowly and unhappy even if I
wished otherwise. *But I have no opinion about this*
because every day I am expecting to be killed or

---

[19] Here St. Patrick refers to his practice of bribing the pagan secu-
lar powers in order to be able to fulfill his mission. Not only did he
not charge people for the administration of the Sacraments, but he
even spent his own money in order to be able to do so.

robbed or reduced to slavery. *But I do not fear* because of the promise of heaven; indeed I throw myself into the hands of the all-powerful God who controls everything. As the Prophet says, "Cast all your cares on the Lord and He will sustain you."

(56) Behold *now I entrust my life to God Who is most faithful* to me, and whose *ambassador I am* in my unworthiness. But He *makes no exception of persons* but chose me for this *as one of the least of His servants.* (57) But *how shall I repay the Lord for His goodness towards me?* What can I promise Him or do for Him considering that without Him I can do nothing? For *He scrutinizes the heart and the intentions* and *I am ready* that He give me *to drink of His chalice* as He has done for the others who loved Him. (58) May God therefore never allow that I lose this *people* that *He has won* at the ends of the earth. I pray to God that He might give me perseverance in my testimony until I pass from this life to Him.

(59) If I have ever done anything good for my God whom I love, I ask Him the grace of shedding my blood for those converts and captives for His name's sake. Because even if I were laid in no tomb and my body was totally mangled by wild dogs or beasts or torn to pieces *by the birds of the air,* I would be full sure that my martyrdom would have saved me body and soul. For on that day we will rise like the brightness of the sun, that is *in the glory* of Christ Jesus our Redeemer. We will be *children* of the living God, *co-heirs with Christ* and *conformed to His future image* for we will reign *through Him, and with Him, and in Him.*

(60) The sun that we see in this life rises daily at His command on our behalf, but the sun will never

reign nor shall its splendor last forever. Those who worship the sun will have a bad end. However, we believe in and worship Christ Who is the true sun and Who will never perish. Likewise anyone who does His will, will not perish but will remain forever. He will reign with the Father and the Holy Spirit, before time and now and for ages of ages. Amen.

(61) Behold, I want to repeat the words of my Confession again and again. In truth *I bear witness in exaltation of heart before God and His holy angels* that I have never had any other motive other than the Gospel to go back to the people from whom I barely escaped.

(62) I beg of those who believe in God and fear Him, that if you decide to read or receive this work of unlearned Patrick which he has written in Ireland, do not credit me with the little I have done according to God's pleasure. Rather conclude, as is indeed true, that anything I achieved was a gift of God. This is my Confession before I die.

2

The Letter of St. Patrick to Coroticus and His Soldiers

This letter was written by St. Patrick in answer to another problem coming from his native Britain. This time it was not spurious accusations that he had to answer, but rather the problem of Coroticus and his soldiers, fellow countrymen of St. Patrick, who had raided Ireland and taken some of his Christian converts as slaves to Britain. St. Patrick knew all too well the hardships of slavery having himself spent years as a slave, so it is natural that he felt a special compassion for these members of his flock. However it was not only human compassion that emboldened him. It was not even concern at the deaths of those who had been slaughtered in the raid; he knew that, as it had happened on the day of their Baptism, they had most likely gone straight to heaven; more importantly, he was worried that the scandalous behavior of Coroticus would harm his mission. Not only did Coroticus give scandal, but also those members of the British Church (even perhaps some of the clergy) who supported him threatened the moral integrity of the Christian message in the Irish mission.

Therefore, St. Patrick sent this open letter to Coroticus and his men, as a kind of writ of excommunication. Here St. Patrick calls for human justice in favor of the enslaved Irish Christians. But the letter ends with a general call to conversion where he offers the possibility of forgiveness and reintegration into the Church to all who repent, regardless of their prior sins.

(1) I, Patrick, an unlearned sinner who dwells in Ireland, profess that I am a bishop. I am sure that it is God *who has made me what I am.* So for the love of God I live among barbarians as a foreigner and exile. God Himself is my witness. I do not wish to say such hard and severe things, but I am compelled to speak by the zeal for God and I am urged by the truth of Christ. I am also urged by the love I have for my neighbors and children, for whom I have *renounced* my fatherland and family and handed over *my very life even unto death.* If I am worthy, I live only for God so that I may teach the pagans even if some despise me.

(2) I have written these words with my own hand so that they can be given and handed over to the soldiers of Coroticus. Because of their evil deeds I am unable to call them my countrymen, or fellow-citizens of the holy Romans[1] for they are fellow-citizens of the demons. Indeed their evil causes them to live in death together with the pagan Irish and apostate Picts.[2] They are covered in blood, the blood from the

---

[1] St. Patrick shows the relationship between Christian faith and the holy Romans, this could refer either to St. Patrick's Roman-British heritage (through which he had been introduced to Christianity) or the link between Christianity itself and the See of Rome.

[2] The Picts were a people who lived in what is today eastern Scotland. They were eventually converted by St. Columba and his monks working from their island-monastery of Iona. The pagan Irish could refer either to the unconverted people of the island or Ireland or, as later

bloodbath they inflicted upon innocent Christians, whom I had won for God by Baptism and Confirmation in Christ.

(3) On the day after their Baptism and Confirmation, when the new Christians were still dressed in white and their foreheads still were fragrant with chrism, they were cruelly slaughtered by these men who put them to the sword.[3] I sent a letter to them with a holy priest whom I had trained from his youth, together with a group of clerics. I begged them to spare us some of their booty by releasing the captured Christians, but they only derided them.[4]

(4) I do not know for whom I should lament more; for those who were killed or for those who were physically enslaved or for those, instead, that the Devil himself has ensnared so terribly.[5] For all eternity they suffer the pains of Gehenna as slaves in the company of the Devil. For *whoever commits sins is a slave* and will be called a *child of the Devil.* (5) Therefore let everyone who fears God know that they are strangers for me and for Christ my God, *whose ambassador I am.* They have killed father and broth-

_____

becomes more apparent, the Irish colonists who had settled in Britain and were to give their name to Scotland (as "Scot" originally meant Irishman).

[3] In accord with ancient liturgical practices, St. Patrick confirmed his new converts with holy chrism in the same celebration as the administration of Baptism.

[4] This present letter is actually the second written by St. Patrick. Here he is referring to the (now lost) first letter addressed directly to Coroticus and his soldiers demanding that they release the Christian slaves and repent of what they had done. As the first private letter had no effect, he is now writing a public letter to these men.

[5] Here St. Patrick contrasts the terrible state of human slavery that the members of his flock had suffered to the even more terrible state of spiritual slavery to the Devil of Coroticus and his soldiers.

er and are *ravenous wolves devouring the people of God as if they were eating bread.* As Scripture says, *O Lord wicked men have destroyed your law,* this law which in recent times has been lovingly planted by God in Ireland where God instructed men in His loving-kindness.

(6) I usurp no man! I have a part with those *who were called and preordained* to announce the Gospel. These preach with no small persecutions *even to the ends of the earth.* I do this preaching in spite of the enemy's jealousy manifested through the tyranny of Coroticus, who shows no respect for God or for His priests, whom He has chosen and filled with the fullness of divine and sublime authority, s*o that whatever they bind on earth will be bound in heaven.*[6]

(7) For these reasons I beg you *holy and humble of heart,* that you not flatter these men. Nor is it permissible *to eat and drink* with them, or even to accept alms from them. This cannot happen unless they first do stringent penance with rivers of tears to make satisfaction to God. They must also free the baptized servants of God and the handmaidens of Christ, on whose behalf He died and was crucified.

(8) *The Most High rejects the gifts of the wicked. Whoever offers a sacrifice taking it from a poor man is like one who sacrifices a son in the presence of the father.* Scripture says that *wealth which has been unjustly gathered will be vomited from his stomach and he will be handed over to the angel of death, the wrath of the dragon will engulf him, he will be slain by the tongue of the viper and the fire which never goes out will consume him.*

---

[6] The enemy that St. Patrick is speaking about is not Coroticus per se but rather the Devil who has deceived Coroticus and is manipulating him to work against St. Patrick's mission.

For this reason, *woe to those who take their fill of what is not their own.* For *what benefit is it for a man to gain the whole world but to lose his soul?* (9) It would be too long here to gather all the texts of the law that deal with such avarice. Avarice is a deadly sin. *You shall not covet your neighbor's goods. You shall not kill,* for a murderer cannot be with Christ. *Whoever hates his brother is a murderer;* it is also written that *he who does not love his brother remains in death.* If this is the case, than how much worse is the plight of those who have drenched their hands in the blood of the children of God; these children that He has recently *gathered* from the ends of the earth by means of our poor preaching.

(10) Is it the case that I came to Ireland without God or *according to the flesh?* Who has forced me? I am *bound by the Spirit* not to see any *of my family.* I myself am not the source of that holy mercy which is offered through me to those people, people who once made a captive of me along with the servants and handmaids of my father's house. *According to the flesh* I was born free, my father was a decurion.[7] I am not ashamed and do not blush to say that I sold my birthright on their behalf. Now I am a slave in Christ for these foreigners because of that ineffable glory of *the eternal life which is in Christ Jesus our Lord.*

(11) If I am not recognized it might be because *a prophet is not honored in his own land.* But it may also be the case *that we are not of the same sheepfold* or that we do not have *God as our common Father.* As Scripture says, *who is not with Me is against Me,*

---

[7] This could refer either to a minor officer in the Roman army or, more likely, to some minor civil position such as a town councilor.

and he who does not gather with Me scatters. We are not in communion; *one destroys while the other builds. I am not looking for my own benefit;* it is not on my own behalf that I speak but on God's. He it is Who has *placed this concern in my heart* that I be one with the *hunters or fisherman* who God prophesied about of old and would come *in these last days.*

(12) What shall I do, O Lord, for they hate me? How much they despise me. Behold, Your sheep around me are being butchered and snatched away by those thieves on the orders of the hostile-minded Coroticus. He is very far from the love of God who betrays the Christians into the hands of the Scots and Picts.[8] *Ravenous wolves* have gobbled up the Lord's flock, which was being well cared for in Ireland and was growing. The sons of the Scots and the daughters of their kings who were becoming monks and virgins for Christ were beyond number. Therefore *the injustice done to the just man is not pleasing to You even as it leads to hell it gives no pleasure.*

(13) Who among the saints would not be horrified at the very thought of enjoying the company of such people or even of sharing a meal with such people?[9] Their houses are full of the booty taken from the dead Christians; they live from pillage. These miserable men do not realize that the food which they offer to their friends and children is in

---

[8] Again it is unclear who these Scots are, but it is likely that they were members of the still-pagan Irish colony in Scotland.

[9] Unfortunately, it would seem that at home Coroticus was seen as a respected member of his local community and maybe even some clerics receive hospitality from him. St. Patrick therefore has to explain to them the consequences of their cooperation.

fact a deadly venom. They are just like Eve who did not realize that she was feeding death to her husband. This is how all evildoers are: *they work death* as an eternal punishment.

(14) The custom of the Roman Christians of Gaul is to send holy men to the Franks and other pagan peoples with thousands of coins in order to redeem baptized captives[10] However you kill them and sell them to a foreign nation that does not know God, it is as if you hand *the members of Christ* over to a whorehouse. What hope can you have in God? Indeed what hope can any have who agrees with you or speaks flattering words to you? God will be the judge. For as Scripture says, *it is not only the evildoers who will be dammed but also those who support them.*

(15) I don't know *what to say* or *what* further *to speak* about those dead children of God who have been cruelly struck by the sword. It is written that we should *weep with those who are weeping* and again *if one member is hurting all the members share in its pain.* Therefore the Church *mourns and weeps for her sons* and daughters who, although they were not yet slain by the sword, were transported to far-off lands where brazen and grave *sins* are easily visible. In these lands freemen have been sold, Christians have been reduced to slavery, and even worse, have become the slaves of the unworthy and dreadful apostate Picts.

---

[10] For many centuries Christians, and monks in particular, used to go into pagan (and later Islamic) lands in order to buy the freedom of those Christians who had been carried there as slaves. St. Patrick places these Gaulish Christians who spend their own money to ransom their fellow Christians from the pagans in stark contrast to Coroticus and his soldiers who actually sell their fellow Christians into slavery.

(16) It is for this reason that I raise my woeful lament: my most loved and delightful brothers and children without number *who I have given birth to in Christ*, what can I do for you; I who am worthy neither to help God nor men? *Wicked men's iniquity has prevailed over us* and *we have become* almost *like foreigners.* Is it that they do not believe that we participate in *one Baptism* or that we have *one God and Father*? They despise us because we are Irish. But Scripture says, *do you not have the same God? Has each one of you abandoned his neighbor?*[11]

(17) Therefore I mourn for you and how I mourn my beloved. But yet I rejoice within myself.[12] I have not *worked* in vain; my pilgrimage has not been *in a total wasteland.* Indeed if this terrible abomination had to happen, thank God, it was as baptized Christians that you departed from this world for paradise. I can behold you, you have started to journey to that place *where night is no more, where there is no more mourning or death, but you will exult like calves who have been freed from their bonds. You shall trample on the wicked who shall be like ashes under your feet.*

(18) You instead will reign with the apostles, the prophets, and the martyrs. You will be received in the eternal kingdom, as God Himself testifies when

---

[11] One of the reasons that Coroticus and his men were accepted in their society was that the Irish were not Roman citizens and therefore were considered as barbarians. St. Patrick counters that what gives Christians their dignity and worth is not simply human citizenship but rather the participation in the Christian faith.

[12] St. Patrick sees that those members of his flock who have been killed by Coroticus have gone to heaven thanks to their recent conversion and their attainment of this destiny is a source of consolation for him.

He says *men will come from east and west and recline with Abraham, and Isaac, and Jacob in the kingdom of heaven. The dogs, and magicians, and murderers will remain outside.* He also says, *the destiny of liars and perjurers shall be the lake of eternal fire.* The Apostle was not wrong when he said that *if it is only with great difficulty that the righteous man will be saved, what shall be the fate of the sinner and the impious transgressor of the law?*

(19) What will happen to Coroticus and his rabble, men who rebel against Christ? What will be the end of these men who distributed young baptized ladies as booty as part of a miserable earthly kingdom which can pass in a single moment? *As clouds or smoke, which is dispersed by the wind* thus fraudulent *sinners* will *perish before the face of the Lord. The just, however, will banquet in security* with Christ and *will judge nations and will dominate* wicked kings forever and ever. Amen.

(20) *I bear witness before God and His angels* that everything I have said will happen even in spite of my lack of expertise, for these are not my own words. No, they belong to God and His Apostles and Prophets, who never tell lies, and I have merely written them down in Latin. *Thus says the Lord. He who believes will be saved, he who does not believe shall be condemned.*

(21) It is my most earnest desire that everyone who serves God may promptly deliver this letter. In this way there will be no chance of it being sent back or hidden from anybody. Rather it should be read aloud and with strength before all peoples, even where Coroticus himself is present. In this

way if God inspires someone *to turn back to God,* he may even at this late stage repent of his most heinous crime, the killing of the Lord's brothers. They can free the baptized women whom they already have taken captive. In this way they will deserve to live with God and be saved now and for all eternity in the peace of the Father, and the Son, and the Holy Spirit. Amen.[13]

---

[13] In an amazing invitation at the end of this letter St. Patrick offers the possibility of repentance and life to Coroticus and his soldiers, showing that it is never too late to repent. Perhaps this sentiment of St. Patrick is the root for the later contribution of the Irish to the Sacrament of Penance or Confession. In the early Church many people were of the opinion that a baptized Christian could only avail of sacramental Penance once in their life. However the current practice of repeatable Penance was popularized by Irish monks in the early Middle Ages. Number 1447 of the *Catechism of the Catholic Church* mentions the contribution of Irish monks to the legitimate development of this doctrine.

St. Patrick

Patrick Francis Cardinal Moran (1830-1911), Archbishop of Sydney

Cardinal Moran was born in Ireland and was orphaned at a young age. He was placed in the care of his uncle Cardinal Cullen who was then rector of the Irish College in Rome. Here the future Cardinal Moran completed his schooling and eventually discerned a vocation to the priesthood. His great academic and personal capacities were soon recognized in Rome and he became a professor at some of the most important Roman universities. Eventually he was named coadjutor bishop of Ossory (located in the South East of Ireland in the counties of Kilkenny, Laois and Offaly). He took part in the First Vatican Council. In 1884 he was transferred to the See of Sydney in Australia where he played a very important role in the establishment of the Church in Australia and also New Zealand. He always retained a love for early Irish ecclesiastical history and wrote many books on the Irish Church and her Saints. This entry in the 1911 edition of the Catholic Encyclopedia *was one of the last works he penned. In addition to St. Patrick's own writings Cardinal Moran relies on ancient biographies of St.*

Patrick (all over 1,000 years old) as well as some details from oral tradition. While modern historians might not agree on each and every detail of Cardinal Moran's presentation, it is generally sound and helps give a fuller picture of St. Patrick and his world and of some of the oldest traditions associated with the Saint.

St. Patrick was Apostle of Ireland, born at Kilpatrick, near Dumbarton, in Scotland, in the year 387; died at Saul, Downpatrick, Ireland, 17 March, 461.

He had for his parents Calphurnius and Conchessa. The former belonged to a Roman family of high rank and held the office of *decurio* in Gaul or Britain. His mother Conchessa was a near relative of the great patron of Gaul, St. Martin of Tours. Kilpatrick still retains many memorials of Saint Patrick, and frequent pilgrimages continued far into the Middle Ages to perpetuate there the fame of his sanctity and miracles.

In his sixteenth year, Patrick was carried off into captivity by Irish marauders and was sold as a slave to a chieftain named Milchu in Dalriada, a territory of the present county of Antrim in Ireland, where for six years he tended his master's flocks in the valley of the Braid and on the slopes of Slemish, near the modern town of Ballymena. He relates in his *Confessio* that during his captivity while tending the flocks he prayed many times in the day: "the love of God," he added, "and His fear increased in me more and more, and the faith grew in me, and the spirit was roused, so that, in a single day, I have said as

many as a hundred prayers, and in the night nearly
the same, so that while in the woods and on the
mountain, even before the dawn, I was roused to
prayer and felt no hurt from it, whether there was
snow or ice or rain; nor was there any slothfulness in
me, such as I see now, because the spirit was then
fervent within me."

In the ways of a benign Providence the six years
of Patrick's captivity became a remote preparation
for his future apostolate. He acquired a perfect
knowledge of the Celtic tongue in which he would
one day announce the glad tidings of Redemption,
and, as his master Milchu was a druidical high
priest, he became familiar with all the details of
Druidism from whose bondage he was destined to
liberate the Irish race.

Admonished by an angel, he, after six years, fled
from his cruel master and bent his steps towards the
west. He relates in his *Confessio* that he had to travel
about 200 miles; and his journey was probably
towards Killala Bay and onwards thence to Westport. He found a ship ready to set sail and after
some rebuffs was allowed on board. In a few days he
was among his friends once more in Britain, but
now his heart was set on devoting himself to the
service of God in the sacred ministry. We meet with
him at St. Martin's monastery at Tours, and again at
the island sanctuary of Lérins which was just then
acquiring widespread renown for learning and piety;
and wherever lessons of heroic perfection in the
exercise of Christian life could be acquired, there
the fervent Patrick was sure to bend his steps. No
sooner had St. Germain entered on his great mission at Auxerre than Patrick put himself under his

guidance, and it was at that great bishop's hands that Ireland's future apostle was a few years later promoted to the priesthood.

It is the tradition in the territory of the Morini that Patrick under St. Germain's guidance for some years was engaged in missionary work among them. When Germain commissioned by the Holy See proceeded to Britain to combat the erroneous teachings of Pelagius, he chose Patrick to be one of his missionary companions and thus it was his privilege to be associated with the representative of Rome in the triumphs that ensued over heresy and paganism, and in the many remarkable events of the expedition, such as the miraculous calming of the tempest at sea, the visit to the relics at St. Alban's shrine, and the Alleluia victory. Amid all these scenes, however, Patrick's thoughts turned towards Ireland, and from time to time he was favored with visions of the children from Focluth, by the Western sea, who cried to him: "O holy youth, come back to Erin, and walk once more among us."

Pope St. Celestine I, who rendered immortal service to the Church by the overthrow of the Pelagian and Nestorian heresies, and by the imperishable wreath of honor decreed to the Blessed Virgin in the General Council of Ephesus, crowned his pontificate by an act of the most far-reaching consequences for the spread of Christianity and civilization, when he entrusted St. Patrick with the mission of gathering the Irish race into the one fold of Christ. Palladius had already received that commission, but terrified by the fierce opposition of a Wicklow chieftain had abandoned the sacred enterprise. It was St. Germain, Bishop of Auxerre, who commended Patrick to the pope. The writer of St. Germain's Life in the ninth century, Heric of Auxerre, thus attests this important fact: "Since the glory of the father shines in the training of the children, of the many sons in Christ whom St. Germain is believed to have had as disciples in religion, let it suffice to make mention here, very briefly, of one most famous, Patrick, the special Apostle of the Irish nation, as the record of his work proves. Subject to that most holy discipleship for 18 years, he drank in no little knowledge in Holy Scripture from the stream of so great a wellspring. Germain sent him, accompanied by Segetius, his priest, to Celestine, Pope of Rome, approved of by whose judgment, supported by whose authority, and strengthened by whose blessing, he went on his way to Ireland."

It was only shortly before his death that Celestine gave this mission to Ireland's apostle and on that occasion bestowed on him many relics and other spiritual gifts, and gave him the name "Patercius" or "Patritius," not as an honorary title, but as a foreshadowing of the fruitfulness and merit of his apostolate whereby he became *pater civium* (the father of his people). Patrick on his return journey from Rome received at Ivrea the tidings of the death of Palladius, and turning aside to the neighboring city of Turin received episcopal consecration at the hands of its great bishop, St. Maximus, and thence hastened on to Auxerre to make under the guidance of St. Germain due preparations for the Irish mission.

It was probably in the summer months of the year 433, that Patrick and his companions landed at the mouth of the Vantry River close by Wicklow Head. The Druids were at once in arms against him. But

Patrick was not disheartened. The intrepid missionary resolved to search out a more friendly territory in which to enter on his mission. First of all, however, he would proceed towards Dalriada, where he had been a slave, to pay the price of ransom to his former master, and in exchange for the servitude and cruelty endured at his hands to impart to him the blessings and freedom of God's children. He rested for some days at the islands off the Skerries coast, one of which still retains the name of Inis-Patrick, and he probably visited the adjoining mainland, which in olden times was known as Holm Patrick. Tradition fondly points out the impression of St. Patrick's foot upon the hard rock—off the main shore, at the entrance to Skerries harbor.

Continuing his course northwards he halted at the mouth of the River Boyne. A number of the natives there gathered around him and heard with joy in their own sweet tongue the glad tidings of Redemption. There too he performed his first miracle on Irish soil to confirm the honor due to the Blessed Virgin, and the Divine birth of our Savior.

Leaving one of his companions to continue the work of instruction so auspiciously begun, he hastened forward to Strangford Loughand there quitting his boat continued his journey over land towards Slemish. He had not proceeded far when a chieftain, named Dichu, appeared on the scene to prevent his further advance. He drew his sword to smite the Saint, but his arm became rigid as a statue and continued so until he declared himself obedient to Patrick. Overcome by the Saint's meekness and miracles, Dichu asked for instruction and made a gift of a large *sabhall* (barn), in which the sacred mysteries were offered up. This was the first sanctuary dedicated by St. Patrick in Erin. It became in later years a chosen retreat of the Saint. A monastery and church were erected there, and the hallowed site retains the name Sabhall (pronounced Saul) to the present day.

Continuing his journey towards Slemish, the Saint was struck with horror on seeing at a distance the fort of his old master Milchu enveloped in flames. The fame of Patrick's marvelous power of miracles preceded him. Milchu, in a fit of frenzy, gathered his treasures into his mansion and setting it on fire, cast himself into the flames. An ancient record adds: "His pride could not endure the thought of being vanquished by his former slave."

Returning to Saul, St. Patrick learned from Dichu that the chieftains of Erin had been summoned to celebrate a special feast at Tara by Leoghaire, who was the Ard-Righ, that is, the Supreme Monarch of Ireland. This was an opportunity which Patrick would not forego; he would present himself before the assembly, to strike a decisive blow against the Druidism that held the nation captive, and to secure freedom for the glad tidings of Redemption of which he was the herald.

As he journeyed on he rested for some days at the house of a chieftain named Secsnen, who with his household joyfully embraced the Faith. The youthful Benen, or Benignus, son of the chief, was in a special way captivated by the Gospel doctrines and the meekness of Patrick. While the Saint slumbered he would gather sweet-scented flowers and scatter them over his bosom, and when Patrick was setting out, continuing his journey towards Tara, Benen clung to his feet declaring that nothing would sever him from him. "Allow him to have his way," said St. Patrick to the chieftain, "he shall be heir to my sacred mission." Thenceforth Benen was the inseparable companion of the Saint, and the prophecy was fulfilled, for Benen is named among the "comhards" or successors of St. Patrick in Armagh.

It was on 26 March, Easter Sunday, in 433, that the eventful assembly was to meet at Tara, and the decree went forth that from the preceding day the fires throughout the kingdom should be extinguished until the signal blaze was kindled at the royal mansion. The chiefs and Brehons came in full numbers and the druids too would muster all their strength to bid defiance to the herald of good tidings and to secure the hold of their superstition on the Celtic race, for their demoniac oracles had announced that the messenger of Christ had come to Erin. St. Patrick arrived at the hill of Slane, at the opposite extremity of the valley from Tara, on Easter Eve, in that year the feast of the Annunciation, and on the summit of the hill kindled the Paschal fire. The druids at once raised their voice. "O King," (they said) "live for ever; this fire, which has been lighted in defiance of the royal edict, will blaze for ever in this land unless it be this very night extinguished." By order of the king and the agency of the druids, repeated attempts were made to extinguish the blessed fire and to punish with death the intruder who had disobeyed the royal command. But the fire was not extinguished and Patrick shielded by the Divine power came unscathed from their snares and assaults.

On Easter Day the missionary band having at their head the youth Benignus bearing aloft a copy of the Gospels, and followed by St. Patrick who with miter and crosier was arrayed in full episcopal attire, proceeded in processional order to Tara. The druids and magicians put forth all their strength and employed all their incantations to maintain their sway over the Irish race, but the prayer and faith of Patrick achieved a glorious triumph. The druids by their incantations overspread the hill and surrounding plain with a cloud of worse then Egyptian darkness. Patrick defied them to remove that cloud, and when all their efforts were made in vain, at his prayer the sun sent forth its rays and the brightest sunshine lit up the scene. Again by demoniac power the Arch-Druid Lochru, like Simon Magus of old, was lifted up high in the air, but when Patrick knelt in prayer the druid from his flight was dashed to pieces upon a rock. Thus was the final blow given to paganism in the presence of all the assembled chieftains. It was, indeed, a momentous day for the Irish race.

Twice Patrick pleaded for the Faith before Leoghaire. The king had given orders that no sign of respect was to be extended to the strangers, but at the first meeting the youthful Erc, a royal page, arose to show him reverence; and at the second, when all the chieftains were assembled, the chief-bard Dubhtach showed the same honor to the Saint. Both these heroic men became fervent disciples of the Faith and bright ornaments of the Irish Church.

It was on this second solemn occasion that St. Patrick is said to have plucked a shamrock from the sward, to explain by its triple leaf and single stem, in some rough way, to the assembled chieftains, the great doctrine of the Blessed Trinity. On that bright Easter Day, the triumph of religion at Tara was complete. The Ard-Righ granted permission to Patrick to preach the Faith throughout the length and breadth of Erin, and the druidical prophecy like the words of Balaam of old would be fulfilled: the sacred fire now kindled by the Saint would never be extinguished.

The beautiful prayer of St. Patrick, popularly known as "St. Patrick's Breastplate," is supposed to have been composed by him in preparation for this victory over Paganism. The following is a literal translation from the old Irish text:

I arise today
Through a mighty strength, the invocation of the Trinity,
Through belief in the threeness,
Through confession of the oneness
Of the Creator of Creation.

I arise today
Through the strength of Christ's birth with His baptism,
Through the strength of His crucifixion with His burial,
Through the strength of His resurrection with His ascension,
Through the strength of His descent for the judgment of Doom.

I arise today
Through the strength of the love of the Cherubim,
In the obedience of angels,
In the service of archangels,
In the hope of the resurrection to meet with reward,
In the prayers of patriarchs,

In prediction of prophets,
In preaching of apostles,
In faith of confessors,
In innocence of holy virgins,
In deeds of righteous men.

I arise today
Through the strength of heaven,
Light of sun,
Radiance of moon,
Splendor of fire,
Speed of lightning,
Swiftness of wind,
Depth of sea,
Stability of earth,
Firmness of rock.

I arise today
Through God's strength to pilot me,
God's might to uphold me,
God's wisdom to guide me,
God's eye to look before me,
God's ear to hear me,
God's word to speak to me,
God's hand to guard me,
God's way to lie before me,
God's shield to protect me,
God's host to save me,
From snares of devils,
From temptation of vices,
From every one who shall wish me ill,
Afar and anear,
Alone and in a multitude.

I summon today all these powers between me and
those evils,

Against every cruel, merciless power that may
  oppose my body and soul,
Against incantations of false prophets,
Against black laws of pagandom,
Against false laws of heretics,
Against craft of idolatry,
Against spells of women, and smiths, and wizards,
Against every knowledge that corrupts man's body
  and soul.

Christ to shield me today,
Against poisoning, against burning,
Against drowning, against wounding,
So there come to me abundance of reward.
Christ with me, Christ before me, Christ behind
  me,
Christ in me, Christ beneath me, Christ above me,
Christ on my right, Christ on my left,
Christ when I lie down, Christ when I sit down,
Christ when I arise,
Christ in the heart of every man who thinks of me,
Christ in the mouth of every one who speaks of me,
Christ in every eye that sees me,
Christ in every ear that hears me.

I arise today
Through a mighty strength, the invocation of the
  Trinity,
Through belief in the threeness,
Through confession of the oneness
Of the Creator of Creation.

[Translator: Kuno Meyer]

St. Patrick remained during Easter week at Slane
and Tara, unfolding to those around him the lessons

of Divine truth. Meanwhile the national games were being celebrated a few miles distant at Tailten (now Telltown) in connection with the royal feast. St. Patrick proceeding there solemnly administered Baptism to Conall, brother of the Ard-Righ Leoghaire, on Wednesday, 5 April. Benen and others had already been privately gathered into the fold of Christ, but this was the first public administering of Baptism, recognized by royal edict, and hence in the ancient Irish calendars to the fifth of April is assigned "the beginning of the Baptism of Erin." This first Christian royal chieftain made a gift to Patrick of a site for a church which to the present day retains the name of Donagh-Patrick. The blessing of heaven was with Conall's family. St. Columba is reckoned among his descendants, and many of the kings of Ireland until the eleventh century were of his race.

St. Patrick left some of his companions to carry on the work of evangelization in Meath, thus so auspiciously begun. He would himself visit the other territories. Some of the chieftains who had come to Tara were from Focluth, in the neighborhood of Killala, in Connaught, and as it was the children of Focluth who in a vision had summoned him to return to Ireland, he resolved to accompany those chieftains on their return, that thus the district of Focluth would be among the first to receive the glad tidings of Redemption.

It affords a convincing proof of the difficulties that St. Patrick had to overcome, that though full liberty to preach the Faith throughout Erin was granted by the monarch of Leoghaire, nevertheless, in order to procure a safe conduct through the inter-

vening territories while proceeding towards
Connaught he had to pay the price of fifteen slaves.
On his way there, passing through Granard he
learned that at Magh-Slecht, not far distant, a vast
concourse was engaged in offering worship to the
chief idol Crom-Cruach. It was a huge stone pillar,
covered with slabs of gold and silver, with a circle of
twelve minor idols around it. He proceeded there,
and with his crosier smote the chief idol that crum-
bled to dust; the others fell to the ground.

At Killala he found the whole people of the territory assembled. At his preaching, the king and his
six sons, with 12,000 of the people, became docile to
the Faith. He spent seven years visiting every district
of Connaught, organizing parishes, forming dioceses, and instructing the chieftains and people.

On the occasion of his first visit to Rathcrogan,
the royal seat of the kings of Connaught, situated
near Tulsk, in the County of Roscommon, a remarkable incident occurred, recorded in many of the
authentic narratives of the Saint's life. Close by the
clear fountain of Clebach, not far from the royal
abode, Patrick and his venerable companions had
pitched their tents and at early dawn were chanting
the praises of the Most High, when the two daughters of the Irish monarch—Ethne, the fair, and
Fedelm, the ruddy—came there, as was their custom, to bathe. Astonished at the vision that present-
ed itself to them, the royal maidens cried out: "Who
are you, and from where do you come? Are you
phantoms, or fairies, or friendly mortals?" St.
Patrick said to them: "It is better if you would adore
and worship the one true God, whom we announce
to you, than that you would satisfy your curiosity by

such vain questions." And then Ethne broke forth into the questions:

Who is God?

And where is God?

Where is His dwelling?

Has He sons and daughters?

Is He rich in silver and gold?

Is He everlasting? Is He beautiful?

Are His daughters dear and lovely to the men of this world?

Is He on the heavens or on earth?

In the sea, in rivers, in mountains, in valleys?

Make Him known to us. How is He to be seen?

How is He to be loved? How is He to be found?

Is it in youth or is it in old age that He may be found?

But St. Patrick, filled with the Holy Ghost, answered:

God, whom we announce to you, is the Ruler of all things.

The God of heaven and earth, of the sea and the rivers.

The God of the sun, and the moon, and all the stars.

The God of the high mountains and of the lowlying valleys.

The God who is above heaven, and in heaven, and under heaven.

His dwelling is in heaven and earth, and the sea, and all therein.

He gives breath to all.

He gives life to all.

He is over all.

He upholds all.

He gives light to the sun.

He imparts splendor to the moon.

He has made wells in the dry land, and islands in the ocean.

He has appointed the stars to serve the greater lights.

His Son is co-eternal and co-equal with Himself.

The Son is not younger than the Father.

And the Father is not older than the Son.

And the Holy Ghost proceeds from them.

The Father, and the Son, and the Holy Ghost are undivided.

But I desire by Faith to unite you to the Heavenly King, as you are daughters of an earthly king.

The maidens, as if with one voice and one heart, said: "Teach us most carefully how we may believe in the Heavenly King; show us how we may behold Him face to face, and we will do whatsoever you shall say to us."

And when he had instructed them he said to them: "Do you believe that by Baptism you put off the sin inherited from the first parents."

They answered: "We believe."

"Do you believe in Penance after sin?"
"We believe."

"Do you believe in life after death? Do you believe in resurrection on the Day of Judgment?"
"We believe."

"Do you believe in the unity of the Church?"
"We believe."

Then they were baptized, and were clothed in white garments. And they beseeched him that they might behold the face of Christ. And the Saint said to them: "You cannot see the face of Christ unless you taste death, and unless you receive the Sacrifice." They answered: "Give us the Sacrifice, so that we may be able to behold our Spouse." And the ancient narrative adds: "when they received the Eucharist of God, they slept in death, and they were placed upon a couch, arrayed in their white baptismal robes."

In 440 St. Patrick entered on the special work of the conversion of Ulster. In the following year, the ancient annalists relate a wonderful spread of the Faith throughout the province. In 444 a site for a church was granted at Armagh by Daire, the chieftain of the district. It was in a valley at the foot of a hill, but the Saint was not content. He had special designs in his heart for that district, and at length the chieftain told him to select in his territory any site he would deem most suitable for his religious purpose. St. Patrick chose that beautiful hill on which the old cathedral of Armagh stands. As he was marking out the church with his companions, they came upon a doe and fawn, and the Saint's companions would have killed them for food; but St. Patrick would not allow them to do so, and, taking the fawn upon his shoulders, and followed by the doe, he proceeded to a neighboring hill, and laid down the fawn, and announced that there, in future times, great glory would be given to the Most High. It was precisely upon that hill thus fixed by St. Patrick that, a few years ago, there was solemnly dedicated the new and beautiful Catholic cathedral of Armagh. A representative of the Holy See presided on the occasion, and hundreds of priests and bishops were gathered there;

and, indeed, it might truly be said, the whole Irish race on that occasion offered up that glorious cathedral to the Most High as tribute to their united faith and piety, and their never-failing love of God.

From Ulster St. Patrick probably proceeded to Meath to consolidate the organization of the communities there, and thence he continued his course through Leinster. Two of the Saint's most distinguished companions, St. Auxilius and St. Iserninus, had the rich valley of the Liffey assigned to them. The former's name is still retained in the church which he founded at Killossy, while the latter is honored as the first Bishop of Kilcullen. As usual, St. Patrick's primary work was to gather the ruling chieftains into the fold. At Naas, the royal residence in those days, he baptized two sons of the King of Leinster. Memorials of the Saint still abound in the district—the ruins of the ancient church which he founded, his holy well, and the hallowed sites in which the power of God was shown forth in miracles. At Sletty, in the immediate neighborhood of Carlow, St. Fiacc, son of the chief Brehon, Dubthach, was installed as bishop, and for a considerable time that See continued to be the chief center of religion for all Leinster. St. Patrick proceeded through Gowran into Ossory; here he erected a church under the invocation of St. Martin, near the present city of Kilkenny, and enriched it with many precious relics which he had brought from Rome.

It was in Leinster, on the borders of the present counties of Kildare and Queen's, that Odhran, St. Patrick's charioteer, attained the martyr's crown. The chieftain of that district honored the demon-idol, Crom Cruach, with special worship, and, on hearing of that idol being cast down, vowed to avenge the insult by the death of our Apostle. Passing through the territory, Odhran overheard the plot that was being organized for the murder of St. Patrick, and as they were setting out in the chariot to continue their journey, asked the Saint, as a favor, to allow him, for the day, to hold the place of honor and rest. This was granted, and scarcely had they set out when a well-directed thrust of a lance pierced the heart of the devoted charioteer, who thus, by changing places, saved St. Patrick's life, and won for himself the martyr's crown.

St. Patrick next proceeded to Munster. As usual, his efforts were directed to combat error in the chief centers of authority, knowing well that, in the paths of conversion, the kings and chieftains would soon be followed by their subjects. At "Cashel of the Kings" he was received with great enthusiasm, the chiefs and Brehons and people welcoming him with joyous acclaim. While engaged in the baptism of the royal prince Aengus, son of the King of Munster, the Saint, leaning on his crosier, pierced with its sharp point the prince's foot. Aengus bore the pain unmoved. When St. Patrick, at the close of the ceremony, saw the blood flow, and asked him why he had been silent, he replied, with genuine heroism, that he thought it might be part of the ceremony, a penalty for the joyous blessings of the Faith that were imparted. The Saint admired his heroism, and, taking the chieftain's shield, inscribed on it a cross with the same point of the crosier, and promised that that shield would be the signal of countless spiritual and temporal triumphs.

Our Apostle spent a considerable time in the present County of Limerick. The fame of his miracles and sanctity had gone before him, and the inhabitants of Thomond and northern Munster, crossing the Shannon in their frail coracles, hastened to receive his instruction. When giving his blessing to them on the summit of the hill of Finnime, looking out on the rich plains before him, he is said to have prophesied the coming of St. Senanus: "To the green island in the West, at the mouth of the sea [i.e., Inis-Cathaigh, now Scattery Island, at the mouth of the Shannon, near Kilrush], the lamp of the people of God will come; he will be the head of counsel to all this territory." At Sangril (now Singland), in Limerick, and also in the district of Garryowen, the holy wells of the Saint are pointed out, and the slab of rock, which served for his bed, and the altar on which every day he offered up the Holy Sacrifice. On the banks of the Suir, and the Blackwater, and the Lee, wherever the Saint preached during the seven years he spent in Munster, a hearty welcome awaited him. An Old Irish life of St. Patrick attests: "After Patrick had founded cells and churches in Munster, and had ordained persons of every grade, and healed the sick, and resuscitated the dead, he bade them farewell, and imparted his blessing to them."

The words of this blessing, which is said to have been given from the hills of Tipperary, as registered in the Saint's Life, to which I have just referred, are particularly beautiful:

A blessing on the Munster people—
Men, youths, and women;

A blessing on the land
That yields them fruit.

A blessing on every treasure
That shall be produced on their plains,
Without any one being in want of help,
God's blessing be on Munster.

A blessing on their peaks,
On their bare flagstones,
A blessing on their glens,
A blessing on their ridges.

Like the sand of the sea under ships,
Be the number in their hearths;
On slopes, on plains,
On mountains, on hills, a blessing.

St. Patrick continued until his death to visit and watch over the churches which he had founded in all the provinces in Ireland. He comforted the faithful in their difficulties, strengthened them in the Faith and in the practice of virtue, and appointed pastors to continue his work among them. It is recorded in his Life that he consecrated no fewer than 350 bishops. He appointed St. Loman to Trim, which rivaled Armagh itself in its abundant harvest of piety. St. Guasach, son of his former master, Milchu, became Bishop of Granard, while the two daughters of the same pagan chieftain founded close by, at Clonbroney, a convent of pious virgins, and merited the aureola of sanctity. St. Mel, nephew of our Apostle, had the charge of Ardagh; St. MacCarthem, who appears to have been particularly loved by St. Patrick, was made Bishop of Clogher.

The narrative in an Old Irish life of Saint Patrick regarding his visit to the district of Costello, in the County of Mayo, serves to illustrate his manner of dealing with the chieftains. He found, it says, the chief, Ernasc, and his son, Loarn, sitting under a tree, "with whom he remained, together with his twelve companions, for a week, and they received from him the doctrine of salvation with attentive ear and mind. Meanwhile he instructed Loarn in the rudiments of learning and piety." A church was erected there, and, years after, Loarn was appointed to its charge.

The manifold virtues by which the early Saints were distinguished shone forth in all their perfection in the life of St. Patrick. When not engaged in the work of the sacred ministry, his whole time was spent in prayer. Many times in the day he armed himself with the sign of the Cross. He never relaxed his penitential exercises. Clothed in a rough hair-shirt, he made the hard rock his bed. His disinterestedness is specially commemorated. Countless converts of high rank would cast their precious ornaments at his feet, but all were restored to them. He had not come to Erin in search of material wealth, but to enrich her with the priceless treasures of the Catholic Faith.

From time to time he withdrew from the spiritual duties of his apostolate to devote himself wholly to prayer and penance. One of his chosen places of solitude and retreat was the island of Lough Derg, which, to this day, has continued to be a favorite resort of pilgrims, and is known as St. Patrick's Purgatory.

Another theater of his miraculous power and piety and penitential austerities in the west of

Ireland merits particular attention. In the far west of Connaught there is a range of tall mountains, which, arrayed in rugged majesty, bid defiance to the waves and storms of the Atlantic. At the head of this range arises a stately cone in solitary grandeur, about 4,000 feet in height, facing Crew Bay, and casting its shadow over the adjoining districts of Aghagower and Westport. This mountain was known in pagan times as the Eagle Mountain, but ever since Ireland was enlightened with the light of Faith it is known as Croagh Patrick, i.e. St. Patrick's mountain, and is honored as the Holy Hill, the Mount Sinai, of Ireland. St. Patrick, in obedience to his guardian Angel, made this mountain his hallowed place of retreat. In imitation of the great Jewish legislator on Sinai, he spent forty days on its summit in fasting and prayer, and other penitential exercises. His only shelter from the fury of the elements, the wind and rain, the hail and snow, was a cave, or recess, in the solid rock; and the flagstone on which he rested his weary limbs at night is still pointed out.

The whole purpose of his prayer was to obtain special blessings and mercy for the Irish race, whom he evangelized. The demons that made Ireland their battlefield mustered all their strength to tempt the Saint and disturb him in his solitude, and turn him away, if possible, from his pious purpose. They gathered around the hill in the form of vast flocks of hideous birds of prey. So dense were their ranks that they seemed to cover the whole mountain, like a cloud, and they so filled the air that Patrick could see neither sky nor earth nor ocean. St. Patrick beseeched God to scatter the demons, but for a time it would seem as if his prayers and tears were in vain.

At length he rang his sweet-sounding bell, symbol of his preaching of the Divine truths. Its sound was heard all over the valleys and hills of Erin, everywhere bringing peace and joy. The flocks of demons began to scatter. He flung his bell among them; they took to precipitate flight, and cast themselves into the ocean. So complete was the Saint's victory over them that, as the ancient narrative adds, "for seven years no evil thing was to be found in Ireland." The Saint, however, would not, as yet, descend from the mountain. He had vanquished the demons, but he would now wrestle with God Himself, like Jacob of old, to secure the spiritual interests of his people.

The Angel had announced to him that, to reward his fidelity in prayer and penance, as many of his people would be gathered into heaven as would cover the land and sea as far as his vision could reach. Far more ample, however, were the aspirations of the Saint, and he resolved to persevere in fasting and prayer until the fullest measure of his petition was granted. Again and again the Angel came to comfort him, announcing new concessions; but all these would not suffice. He would not relinquish his post on the mountain, or relax his penance, until all were granted. At length the message came that his prayers were heard: many souls would be free from the pains of purgatory through his intercession; whoever in the spirit of penance would recite his hymn before death would attain the heavenly reward; barbarian hordes would never obtain sway in his Church; seven years before the Judgment Day, the sea would spread over Ireland to save its people from the temptations and terrors of the Antichrist; and greatest blessing of all, Patrick himself should be deputed to judge the whole Irish race on the last day.

Such were the extraordinary favors which St. Patrick, with his wrestling with the Most High, his unceasing prayers, his unconquerable love of heavenly things, and his unremitting penitential deeds, obtained for the people whom he evangelized.

It is sometimes supposed that St. Patrick's apostolate in Ireland was an unbroken series of peaceful triumphs, and yet it was quite the reverse. No storm of persecution was, indeed stirred up to assail the infant Church, but the Saint himself was subjected to frequent trials at the hands of the druids and of other enemies of the Faith. He tells us in his *Confessio* that no fewer than twelve times he and his companions were seized and carried off as captives, and on one occasion in particular he was loaded with chains, and his death was decreed. But from all these trials and sufferings he was liberated by a benign Providence. It is on account of the many hardships which he endured for the Faith that, in some of the ancient Martyrologies, he is honored as a martyr.

St. Patrick, having now completed his triumph over paganism, and gathered Ireland into the fold of Christ, prepared for the summons to his reward. St. Brigid came to him with her chosen virgins, bringing the shroud in which he would be enshrined. It is recorded that when St. Patrick and St. Brigid were united in their last prayer, a special vision was shown to him. He saw the whole of Ireland lit up with the brightest rays of Divine Faith. This continued for centuries, and then clouds gathered around the devoted island, and, little by little, the religious glory faded away, until, in the course of centuries, it was only in the remotest valleys that some glimmer of its light remained. St. Patrick prayed that the light would never be extinguished, and, as he prayed, the Angel came to him and said: "Fear not: your apostolate shall never cease." As he thus prayed, the glimmering light grew in brightness, and ceased not until once more all the hills and valleys of Ireland were lit up in their pristine splendor, and then the Angel announced to St. Patrick: "Such shall be the abiding splendor of Divine truth in Ireland."

At Saul (Sabhall), St. Patrick received the summons to his reward on 17 March, 461. St. Tassach administered the last Sacraments to him. His remains were wrapped in the shroud woven by St. Brigid's own hands. The bishops and clergy and faithful people from all parts crowded around his remains to pay due honor to the Father of their Faith. Some of the ancient Lives record that for several days the light of heaven shone around his bier. His remains were interred at the chieftain's Dun or Fort two miles from Saul, where in later years arose the cathedral of Down.

– 4 –

Pope John Paul II

On my knees I beg you to
turn away from violence

The following is the text of Pope John Paul II's homily at Killineer, near Drogheda, County Louth, on Saturday, October 29th, 1979. On the occasion of Pope John Paul II's apostolic visit to Ireland (the first such visit to Ireland by any Pope) the Pope desired to make a pilgrimage to Armagh whose Archbishop is the successor of St. Patrick. However the political situation in the North of Ireland (where Armagh is located) made such a visit impossible. Therefore the Pope celebrated Mass with 300,000 of the faithful in attendance near Drogheda, a town in the Republic which is within the Archdiocese of Armagh and near the border. This pilgrimage had great meaning for the Pope himself and here he also strongly exhorted the people of Ireland to work for peace and justice.

Dear brothers and sisters in Jesus Christ,

Having greeted the soil of Ireland today on my arrival in Dublin, I make my first Irish journey to this place, to Drogheda. The cry of centuries sends me here.

I arrive as a pilgrim of faith, I arrive also as successor of Peter, to whom Christ has given a particular care for the universal Church. I desire to visit those places in Ireland, in particular, where the power of God and the action of the Holy Spirit have been specially manifested. I seek first those places which carry in themselves the sign of the "beginning;" and "beginning" is connected with "firstness," with primacy. Such a place on Irish soil is Armagh, for centuries the Episcopal See of the Primate of Ireland.

The Primate is he who has the first place among the bishops, shepherds of the People of God in this land. This primacy is linked to the "beginning" of the faith, and of the Church in this country. That is to say, it is linked to the heritage of Saint Patrick, patron of Ireland.

Hence, I desired to make my first Irish journey a journey towards the "beginning," the place of the primacy. The Church is built in her entirety on the foundation of the Apostles and Prophets, Christ Jesus himself being the chief cornerstone (see Eph 2:20). But, in each land and nation the Church has her own particular foundation stone. So, it is towards this foundation here in the Primatial See of Armagh that I first direct my pilgrim steps. The See of Armagh is the Primatial See, because it is the See of Saint Patrick. The Archbishop of Armagh is Primate of all Ireland today because he is the *Comharba Phadraig,* the successor of Saint Patrick, the first Bishop of Armagh.

Standing for the first time on Irish soil, on Armagh soil, the Successor of Peter cannot but recall the first coming here, more than 1,500 years ago, of Saint Patrick.

From his days as a shepherd boy at Slemish right up to his death at Saul, Patrick was a witness to Jesus Christ. Not far from this spot, on the Hill of Slane, it is said that he lit, for the first time in Ireland, the Paschal Fire so that the light of Christ might shine forth on all of Ireland and unite all of its people in the love of the one Jesus Christ.

It gives me great joy to stand here with you today, within sight of Slane, and to proclaim this same Jesus, the Incarnate Word of God, the Savior of the world. He is the Lord of history, the Light of the world, the Hope of the future of all humanity. In the words of the Easter liturgy, celebrated for the first time in Ireland by Saint Patrick on the hill of Slane, we greet Christ today: He is the Alpha and the Omega, the beginning of all things and their end. All time is His, and all the ages. To Him be glory for ever and ever. *Lumen Christi: Deo Gratias.* The Light of Christ: Thanks be to God. May the light of Christ, the light of faith, continue always to shine out from Ireland. May no darkness ever be able to extinguish it.

That he might be faithful to the end of his life to the light of Christ was Saint Patrick's prayer for himself. That the people of Ireland might remain faithful always to the light of Christ was his constant prayer for the Irish. He wrote in his *Confession*:

"May God never permit it to happen to me that I should lose His people that He purchased in the utmost parts of the world. I pray to God to give me perseverance, and to deign that I be a faithful witness to Him to the end of my life for God . . . From time to time I came to know Him in my youth, the love of God and the fear of Him have grown in me, and up to now, thanks to the grace of God, I have kept the faith" (*Confession* 44, 58).

"I have kept the faith." That has been the ambition of the Irish down the centuries. Through persecution and through poverty, in famine and in exile, you have kept faith. For many it has meant martyrdom. Here at Drogheda, where his relics are honored, I wish to mention one Irish martyr, Saint Oliver Plunkett, at whose canonization in the Holy Year 1975, I was happy to assist, as Cardinal of Cracow, on the invitation of my friend, the late Cardinal Conway.

Saint Oliver Plunkett, Primate of Ireland for twelve years, is forever an outstanding example of the love of Christ for all men. As bishop, he preached a message of pardon and peace. He was, indeed, the defender of the oppressed and the advocate of justice, but he would never condone violence. For men of violence, his word was the word of the Apostle Peter: "Never pay back one wrong with another" (1 Pet 3:9). As a martyr for the faith, he sealed by his death the same message of reconciliation that he had preached during his life. In his heart there was no rancor, for his strength was the love of Jesus, the love of the Good Shepherd who gives His life for His flock. His dying words were words of forgiveness for all His enemies.

Faith and fidelity are the marks of the Church in Ireland, a Church of martyrs, a Church of Witnesses; a Church of heroic faith, heroic fidelity. These are the historical signs marking the track of faith on Irish soil. The Gospel and the Church have struck deep roots in the soul of the Irish people.

The See of Armagh, the See of Patrick, is the place to see that track, to feel those roots. It is the place in which to meet, from which to address, those other great and faithful dioceses whose people have suffered so much from the events of the past decade,

Down and Connor, Derry, Dromore, Clogher, Kilmore.

During the period and preparation of my visit to Ireland, especially precious to me was the invitation of the Primate of all Ireland that I should visit his cathedral in Armagh. Particularly eloquent, also, was the fact that the invitation of the Primate was taken up and repeated by the representatives of the Church of Ireland, and by leaders and members of the other Churches, including many from Northern Ireland. For all these invitations, I am particularly grateful.

These invitations are an indication of the fact that the Second Vatican Council is achieving its work, and that we are meeting with our fellow-Christians of other Churches as people who together confess Jesus Christ as Lord, and who are drawing closer to one another in Him as we search for unity and common witness.

This truly fraternal and ecumenical act on the part of representatives of the Churches is also a testimony that the tragic events taking place in Northern Ireland do not have their source in the fact of belonging to different Churches and Confessions; that this is not—despite what is so often repeated before world opinion—a religious war, a struggle between Catholics and Protestants. On the contrary, Catholics and Protestants, as people who confess Christ, taking inspiration from their faith and the Gospel, are seeking to draw closer to one another in unity and peace. When they recall the greatest commandment of Christ, the commandment of love, they cannot behave otherwise.

But Christianity does not command us to close our eyes to difficult human problems. It does not permit us to neglect and refuse to see unjust social, or international situations. What Christianity does forbid is to seek solutions to these situations by the ways of hatred, by the murdering of defenseless people, by the methods of terrorism. Let me say more: Christianity understands and recognizes the noble and just struggle for justice; but Christianity is decisively opposed to fomenting hatred and to promoting or provoking violence or struggle for the sake of "struggle." The command, "Thou shalt not kill," must be binding on the conscience of humanity, if the terrible tragedy and destiny of Cain is not to be repeated.

For this reason it was fitting for me to come here before going to America, where I hope to address the United Nations Organization on these same problems of peace and war, justice and human rights. We have decided together, the Cardinal Primate and I, that it would be better for me to come here, to Drogheda, and that it should be from here that I would render homage to the "beginning" of the faith, and to the primacy in your homeland; and from here that I should reflect with all of you, before God, before your splendid Christian history, on this most urgent problem, the problem of peace and reconciliation.

We must, above all, clearly realize where the causes of this dramatic struggle are found. We must call by name those systems and ideologies that are responsible for this struggle. We must also reflect whether the ideology of subversion is the true good of your people, for the true good of man. Is it possible to construct the good of individuals and peoples on hatred, on war? Is it right to push the young generations into the pit of fratricide? Is it not necessary to seek solutions to our problems by a different way? Does not the fratricidal struggle make it even more urgent for us to seek peaceful solutions with all our energies?

These questions I shall be discussing before the United Nations Assembly in a few days. Here today, in this beloved land of Ireland, from which so many before me have departed for America, I wish to discuss them with you.

My message to you today cannot be different from what Saint Patrick and Saint Oliver Plunkett taught you. I preach, what they preach: Christ, Who is the "Prince of Peace" (Is 9:5), who reconciled us to God and to each other (see 2 Cor 5:18), Who is the source of all unity.

The Gospel reading of this Mass tells us of Jesus as the "the Good Shepherd," whose one desire is to bring all together in one flock. I come to you in His name, in the name of Jesus Christ, Who died in order "to gather into one, the children of God who are scattered abroad" (Jn 11:52). This is my mission, my message to you: Jesus Christ Who is our peace. Christ "is our peace" (Eph 2:11). And today and forever He repeats to us: "My peace I give to you, My peace I leave with you" (Jn 14:27). Never before in the history of mankind has peace been so much talked about and so ardently desired as in our day.

The growing interdependence of peoples and nations makes almost everyone subscribe—at least in principle—to the ideal of universal human brotherhood. Great international institutions debate humanity's peaceful coexistence. Public opinion is growing in consciousness of the absurdity of war as a means to resolve differences. More and more, peace is seen as a necessary condition for fraternal relations among nations, and among peoples.

Peace is more and more clearly seen as the only way to justice; peace is itself the work of justice. And yet again, and again, one can see how peace is undermined and destroyed. Why is it then that our convictions do not always match our behavior and our attitudes? Why is it that we do not seem to be able to banish all conflicts from our lives?

Peace is the result of many converging attitudes and realities: it is the product of moral concerns, of ethical principles based on the Gospel message and fortified by it.

I want to mention here in the first place: justice. In his message for the 1971 Day of Peace, my revered predecessor, that Pilgrim for peace, Paul VI, said: "True peace must be founded upon justice, upon a sense of the untouchable dignity of man, upon the recognition of an indelible and happy equality between men, upon the basic principle of human brotherhood, that is, of the respect and love due to each man, because he is man."

This same message I affirmed in Mexico and in Poland. I reaffirm it here in Ireland. Every human being has inalienable rights that must be respected. Each human community—ethnic, historical, cultural or religious—has rights which must be respected. Peace is threatened every time one of these rights is violated. The moral law, guardian of human rights, protector of the dignity of man, cannot be set aside by any person or group, or by the State itself, for any cause, not even for security or in the interests of law and order. The Law of God stands in judgment over all reasons of State.

As long as injustice exists in any of the areas that touch upon the dignity of the human person, be it in the political, social or economic field, be it in the cultural or religious sphere, true peace will not exist. The causes of inequalities must be identified through a courageous and objective evaluation, and they must be eliminated so that every person can develop and grow in the full measure of his or her humanity.

Secondly, peace cannot be established by violence, peace can never flourish in a climate of terror, intimidation and death. It is Jesus Himself Who said: "All who take the sword will perish by the sword" (Mt 26:52). This is the word of God, and it commands this generation of violent men to desist from hatred and violence and to repent.

I join my voice today to the voice of Paul VI and my other predecessors, to the voices of your religious leaders, to the voices of all men and women of reason, and I proclaim, with the conviction of my faith in Christ and with an awareness of my mission, that violence is evil, that violence is unacceptable as a solution to problems, that violence is unworthy of man.

Violence is a lie, for it goes against the truth of our faith, the truth of our humanity. Violence destroys what it claims to defend: the dignity, the life, the freedom of human beings. Violence is a crime against humanity, for it destroys the very fabric of society. I pray with you that the moral sense and Christian conviction of Irish men and women may never become obscured and blunted by the lie of violence, that nobody may ever call murder by any other name than murder, that the spiral of violence may never be given the distinction of unavoidable logic or necessary retaliation. Let us remember that the word remains for ever; "All who take the sword will perish by the sword."

There is another word that must be part of the vocabulary of every Christian, especially when barriers of hate and mistrust have been constructed. This is reconciliation. "So if you are offering your gift at the altar, and there remember that your brother has something against you, leave your gift there before the altar and go: be reconciled with your brother and then come out and offer your gift" (Mt 5:23–24).

This command of Jesus is stronger than any barrier that human inadequacy or malice can build. Even when our belief in the fundamental goodness of every human being has been shaken or undermined, even if longer-held convictions and attitudes have hardened our hearts, there is one source of power that is stronger than every disappointment, bitterness or ingrained mistrust, and that power is Jesus Christ, who brought forgiveness and reconciliation to the world.

I appeal to all who listen to me; to all who are discouraged after the many years of strife, violence and alienation—that they attempt the seemingly impossible to put an end to the intolerable. I pay homage to the many efforts that have been made by countless men and women in Northern Ireland to walk the path of reconciliation and peace.

The courage, the patience, the indomitable hope for the men and women of peace have lighted up the darkness of these years of trial. The spirit of Christian forgiveness shown by so many who have suffered in their persons or through their loved ones have given inspiration to multitudes. In the years to come, when the words of hatred and the deeds of violence are forgotten, it is the words of love and the acts of peace and forgiveness which will be remembered. It is these which will inspire the generations to come.

To all of you who are listening I say: do not believe in violence; do not support violence. It is not the Christian way. It is not the way of the Catholic Church. Believe in peace and forgiveness and love; for they are of Christ.

Communities who stand together in their acceptance of Jesus' supreme message of love, expressed in peace and reconciliation, and in their rejection of all violence, constitute an irresistible force for achieving what many have come to accept as impossible and destined to remain so.

Now I wish to speak to all men and women engaged in violence. I appeal to you, in language of passionate pleading. On my knees, I beg you to turn away from the paths of violence and to return to the ways of peace. You may claim to seek justice. I, too, believe in justice, and seek justice. But violence only delays the day of justice. Violence destroys the work of justice. Further violence in Ireland will only drag down to ruin the land you claim to love and the values you claim to cherish.

In the name of God I beg you: return to Christ, Who died so that men might live in forgiveness and peace. He is waiting for you, longing for each one of you to come to Him so that He may say to each of you: your sins are forgiven; go in peace.

I appeal to young people who may have become caught up in organizations engaged in violence, I say to you, with all the love I have for you, with all the trust I have in young people: do not listen to voices which speak the language of hatred, revenge, retaliation. Do not follow any leaders who train you in the ways of inflicting death. Love life; respect life; in yourselves and in others. Give yourselves to the service of life, not the work of death.

Do not think that courage and strength are proved by killing and destruction. The true courage lies in working for peace. The true strength lies in joining with the young men and women of your generation everywhere in building up a just and human and Christian society by the ways of peace. Violence is the enemy of justice. Only peace can lead the way to true justice.

My dear young people; if you have been caught up in the ways of violence, even if you have done deeds of violence, come back to Christ, whose parting gift to the world was peace. Only when you come back to Christ, will you find peace for your troubled consciences and rest for your disturbed souls.

And, to you, fathers and mothers, I say: Teach your children how to forgive, make your homes places of love and forgiveness; make your streets and neighborhoods centers of peace and reconciliation. It would be a crime against youth, and their future, to let even one child grow up with nothing but the experience of violence and hate.

Now, I wish to speak to all the people in positions of leadership, to all who can influence public opinion, to all members of political parties and to all who support them. I say to you:

Never think you are betraying your own community by seeking to understand and respect and accept those of a different tradition. You will serve your own tradition best by working for reconciliation with others.

Each of the historical communities in Ireland can only harm itself by seeking to harm the other. Continued violence can only endanger everything that is most precious in the traditions and aspirations of both communities.

Let no one concerned with Ireland have any illusions about the nature and the menace of political violence. The ideology and the methods of violence have become an international problem of the utmost gravity. The longer the violence continues in Ireland, the more the danger will grow that this beloved land could become yet another theater for international terrorism.

To all who bear political responsibility for the affairs of Ireland, I want to speak with the same urgency and intensity with which I have spoken to the men of violence. Do not cause, or condone, or tolerate, conditions which give excuse, or pretext, to men of violence.

For those who resort to violence always claim that only violence brings about change. They claim that political action cannot achieve justice. You, politicians, must prove them to be wrong. You must show that there is a peaceful, political way to justice. You must show that peace achieves the works of justice, and violence does not.

I urge you who are called to the noble vocation of politics to have the courage to face up to your responsibility, to be leaders in the cause of peace, reconciliation and justice. If politicians do not decide and act for just change, then the field is left open to the men of violence. Violence thrives best when there is political vacuum and a refusal of political movement.

Paul VI, writing to Cardinal Conway in March, 1972, said: "Everyone must play his part. Obstacles which stand in the way of justice must be removed: obstacles such as civil inequity, social and political discrimination, and misunderstanding between individuals and groups. There must be a mutual and abiding respect for others: for their persons, their rights and their lawful aspirations." I make these words of my revered predecessor my own today.

I came to Drogheda today on a great mission of peace and reconciliation. I come as a pilgrim of peace, Christ's peace. To Catholics, to Protestants, my message is peace and love. May no Irish Protestant think that the Pope is an enemy, a danger or a threat. My desire is that instead Protestants would see in me a friend and a brother in Christ. Do not lose trust that this visit of mine may be fruitful, that this voice of mine may be listened to. And, even if it were not listened to, let history record that at a difficult moment in the experience of the people of Ireland, the Bishop of Rome set foot in your land, that he was with you and prayed with you for peace and reconciliation, for the victory of justice and love over hatred and violence. Yes, this, our witness, finally becomes a prayer, a prayer from the heart for peace for the peoples who live on this earth, peace for all the people of Ireland.

Let this fervent prayer for peace penetrate with light all consciences. Let it purify them and take hold of them.

Christ, Prince of Peace; Mary, Mother of Peace, Queen of Ireland; Saint Patrick, Saint Oliver, and all Saints of Ireland; I, together with all those gathered here and with all who join with me, invoke you, watch over Ireland. Protect humanity. Amen.

A Novena to St. Patrick

Inspired by the High Cross at Moone, Co. Kildare, Ireland

by

Fr. Neil Xavier O'Donoghue

This novena uses two prayers traditionally ascribed to St. Patrick. The first is called "St. Patrick's Breastplate" and is in the form of a litany that was popular in early Christian Ireland. The second prayer in this Novena has been modified from a section of Tírechán's Collectanea, *one of the earliest biographies of St. Patrick. Tírechán tells how one day at Rathcrogan, County Roscommon, St. Patrick met two princesses Ethne and Fedelm, daughters of the King of Connaught. These two asked the saint to explain who his God was and the prayer has been based on his description of God to them.*

In order to give a daily theme to the Novena, I have taken inspiration from the High Cross at Moone, County Kildare. High Crosses were built in many Irish Church centers with many of the surviving crosses being erected in the ninth and tenth centuries. Oftentimes these High Crosses depict Biblical scenes and the Cross of Moone is a particularly good example of this type. Eleven individual carvings have been identified on this Cross and nine of them, including two Crucifixion scenes, have been identified as Biblical (the other two are scenes from the life of St. Anthony of the Desert, the father of monasticism).[1] *Although some of the carvings are a little worn having endured a millennium of Irish rain, they still evoke the Biblical catechesis of the early Irish Church.*

Day One: Adam and Eve

Breastplate of St. Patrick

I arise today
Through a mighty strength, the invocation of the
    Trinity,
Through belief in the threeness,
Through confession of the oneness
Of the Creator of Creation.

I arise today
Through the strength of Christ's birth with His
    baptism,
Through the strength of His crucifixion with His
    burial,
Through the strength of His resurrection with His
    ascension,
Through the strength of His descent for the judgment of Doom.

---

[1] Photographs by Fr. Neil Xavier O'Donoghue/Joe Polillio Photography.

I arise today
Through the strength of the love of the Cherubim,
In the obedience of angels,
In the service of archangels,
In the hope of the resurrection to meet with reward,
In the prayers of patriarchs,
In prediction of prophets,
In preaching of apostles,
In faith of confessors,
In innocence of holy virgins,
In deeds of righteous men.

I arise today
Through the strength of heaven,
Light of sun,
Radiance of moon,
Splendor of fire,
Speed of lightning,
Swiftness of wind,
Depth of sea,
Stability of earth,
Firmness of rock.

I arise today
Through God's strength to pilot me,
God's might to uphold me,
God's wisdom to guide me,
God's eye to look before me,
God's ear to hear me,
God's word to speak to me,
God's hand to guard me,
God's way to lie before me,
God's shield to protect me,
God's host to save me,

From snares of devils,
From temptation of vices,
From every one who shall wish me ill,
Afar and anear,
Alone and in a multitude.

I summon today all these powers between me and
those evils,
Against every cruel, merciless power that may
oppose my body and soul,
Against incantations of false prophets,
Against black laws of pagandom,
Against false laws of heretics,
Against craft of idolatry,
Against spells of women, and smiths, and wizards,
Against every knowledge that corrupts man's body
and soul.

Christ to shield me today,
Against poisoning, against burning,
Against drowning, against wounding,
So there come to me abundance of reward.
Christ with me, Christ before me, Christ behind
me,
Christ in me, Christ beneath me, Christ above me,
Christ on my right, Christ on my left,
Christ when I lie down, Christ when I sit down,
Christ when I arise,
Christ in the heart of every man who thinks of me,
Christ in the mouth of every one who speaks of me,
Christ in every eye that sees me,
Christ in every ear that hears me.

I arise today
Through a mighty strength, the invocation of the
Trinity,

Through belief in the threeness,
Through confession of the oneness
Of the Creator of Creation.

[Translator: Kuno Meyer]

Biblical Reading: Genesis 3:1-13

Now the serpent was more crafty than any other wild animal that the LORD God had made. He said to the woman, "Did God say, 'You shall not eat from any tree in the garden'?" The woman said to the serpent, "We may eat of the fruit of the trees in the garden; but God said, 'You shall not eat of the fruit of the tree that is in the middle of the garden, nor shall you touch it, or you shall die.' " But the serpent said to the woman, "You will not die; for God knows that when you eat of it your eyes will be opened, and you will be like God, knowing good and evil." So when the woman saw that the tree was good for food, and that it was a delight to the eyes, and that the tree was to be desired to make one wise, she took of its fruit and ate; and she also gave some to her husband, who was with her, and he ate. Then the eyes of both were opened, and they knew that they were naked; and they sewed fig leaves together and made loincloths for themselves.

They heard the sound of the LORD God walking in the garden at the time of the evening breeze, and the man and his wife hid themselves from the presence of the LORD God among the trees of the garden. But the LORD God called to the man, and said to him, "Where were you?" He said, "I heard the sound of you in the garden, and I was afraid, because I was naked; and I hid myself." He said,

"Who told you that you were naked? Have you eaten from the tree of which I commanded you not to eat?" The man said, "The woman whom you gave to be with me, she gave me the fruit from the tree, and I ate." Then the LORD God said to the woman, "What is it that you have done?" The woman said, "The serpent tricked me, and I ate."

Novena Prayer

Our God, You are the God of all people.
You are the God of Heaven and earth, the God of the sea and the rivers, the God of the sun and the moon and all the stars, the God of the high mountains and the deep valleys.
O God, You are above the heavens, and in the heavens, and below the heavens.
You dwell in the heavens and on the earth, and in the sea, and in all the places therein.
You inspire all things, You give life to all things, You are above all things, You are below all things.
You give the sun its light,
You give the night and the stars their light,
You make springs of water in the desert and dry islands in the sea,
and You make the stars to serve the greater lights.
You have a Son Who is co-eternal with Yourself, and like Yourself in every way;
Your Son is no younger than You, O Father, nor are You, O Father, older than Your Son, and the Holy Spirit breathes through both the Father and the Son, and You, O God, are one, Father, Son, and Holy Spirit.

In the name of St. Patrick, Apostle of Ireland, I place my prayer before You and ask that, through his intercession You may grant my petition that *[name your petition here]* if it be according to Your will.

Day 2: The Sacrifice of Isaac

Breastplate of St. Patrick

I arise today
Through a mighty strength, the invocation of the
    Trinity,
Through belief in the threeness,
Through confession of the oneness
Of the Creator of Creation.

I arise today
Through the strength of Christ's birth with His
    baptism,
Through the strength of His crucifixion with His
    burial,
Through the strength of His resurrection with His
    ascension,
Through the strength of His descent for the judg-
    ment of Doom.

I arise today
Through the strength of the love of the Cherubim,

In the obedience of angels,
In the service of archangels,
In the hope of the resurrection to meet with re-
    ward,
In the prayers of patriarchs,
In prediction of prophets,
In preaching of apostles,
In faith of confessors,
In innocence of holy virgins,
In deeds of righteous men.

I arise today
Through the strength of heaven,
Light of sun,
Radiance of moon,
Splendor of fire,
Speed of lightning,
Swiftness of wind,
Depth of sea,
Stability of earth,
Firmness of rock.

I arise today
Through God's strength to pilot me,
God's might to uphold me,
God's wisdom to guide me,
God's eye to look before me,
God's ear to hear me,
God's word to speak to me,
God's hand to guard me,
God's way to lie before me,
God's shield to protect me,
God's host to save me,
From snares of devils,
From temptation of vices,

From every one who shall wish me ill,
Afar and anear,
Alone and in a multitude.

I summon today all these powers between me and
    those evils,
Against every cruel, merciless power that may
    oppose my body and soul,
Against incantations of false prophets,
Against black laws of pagandom,
Against false laws of heretics,
Against craft of idolatry,
Against spells of women, and smiths, and wizards,
Against every knowledge that corrupts man's body
    and soul.

Christ to shield me today,
Against poisoning, against burning,
Against drowning, against wounding,
So there come to me abundance of reward.
Christ with me, Christ before me, Christ behind
    me,
Christ in me, Christ beneath me, Christ above me,
Christ on my right, Christ on my left,
Christ when I lie down, Christ when I sit down,
Christ when I arise,
Christ in the heart of every man who thinks of me,
Christ in the mouth of every one who speaks of me,
Christ in every eye that sees me,
Christ in every ear that hears me.

I arise today
Through a mighty strength, the invocation of the
    Trinity,
Through belief in the threeness,

Through confession of the oneness
Of the Creator of Creation.

[Translator: Kuno Meyer]

Biblical Reading: Genesis 22:1-14

After these things God tested Abraham. He said to
him, "Abraham!" And he said, "Here I am!" He said,
"Take your son, your only son Isaac, whom you love,
and go to the land of Moriah, and offer him there as
a burnt offering on one of the mountains that I shall
show you." So Abraham rose early in the morning,
saddled his donkey, and took two of his young men
with him, and his son Isaac; he cut the wood for the
burnt offering, and set out and went to the place in
the distance that God had shown him. On the third
day Abraham looked up and saw the place far away.
Then Abraham said to his young men, "Stay here
with the donkey; the boy and I will go over there; we
will worship, and then we will come back to you."
Abraham took the wood of the burnt offering and laid
it on his son Isaac, and he himself carried the fire and
the knife. So the two of them walked on together.
Isaac said to his father Abraham, "Father!" And he
said, "Here I am, my son." He said, "The fire and the
wood are here, but where is the lamb for a burnt
offering?" Abraham said, "God himself will provide
the lamb for a burnt offering, my son." So the two of
them walked on together.

When they came to the place that God had shown
him, Abraham built an altar there and laid the wood
in order. He bound his son Isaac, and laid him on the
altar, on top of the wood. Then Abraham reached out
his hand and took the knife to kill his son. But the
angel of the LORD called to him from heaven, and
said, "Abraham, Abraham!" And he said, "Here I

am." He said, "Do not lay your hand on the boy or do anything to him; for now I know that you fear God, since you have not withheld your son, your only son, from me." And Abraham looked up and saw a ram, caught in a thicket by its horns. Abraham went and took the ram and offered it up as a burnt offering instead of his son. So Abraham called that place, "The LORD will provide"; as it is said to this day, "On the mount of the Lord it shall be provided."

Novena Prayer

Our God, You are the God of all people.

You are the God of Heaven and earth, the God of the sea and the rivers, the God of the sun and the moon and all the stars, the God of the high mountains and the deep valleys.

O God, You are above the heavens, and in the heavens, and below the heavens.

You dwell in the heavens and on the earth, and in the sea, and in all the places therein.

You inspire all things, You give life to all things, You are above all things, You are below all things.

You give the sun its light,

You give the night and the stars their light,

You make springs of water in the desert and dry islands in the sea,

and You make the stars to serve the greater lights.

You have a Son Who is co-eternal with Yourself, and like Yourself in every way;

Your Son is no younger than You, O Father, nor are You, O Father, older than Your Son, and the Holy Spirit breathes through both the Father and the Son, and You, O God, are one, Father, Son, and Holy Spirit.

In the name of St. Patrick, Apostle of Ireland, I place my prayer before You and ask that, through his intercession You may grant my petition that *[name your petition here]* if it be according to Your will.

Day 3: Daniel in the Lions' Den

Breastplate of St. Patrick

I arise today
Through a mighty strength, the invocation of the Trinity,
Through belief in the threeness,
Through confession of the oneness
Of the Creator of Creation.

I arise today
Through the strength of Christ's birth with His baptism,
Through the strength of His crucifixion with His burial,
Through the strength of His resurrection with His ascension,
Through the strength of His descent for the judgment of Doom.

I arise today
Through the strength of the love of the Cherubim,
In the obedience of angels,
In the service of archangels,
In the hope of the resurrection to meet with reward,
In the prayers of patriarchs,
In prediction of prophets,
In preaching of apostles,
In faith of confessors,
In innocence of holy virgins,
In deeds of righteous men.

I arise today
Through the strength of heaven,
Light of sun,
Radiance of moon,
Splendor of fire,
Speed of lightning,
Swiftness of wind,
Depth of sea,
Stability of earth,
Firmness of rock.

I arise today
Through God's strength to pilot me,
God's might to uphold me,
God's wisdom to guide me,
God's eye to look before me,
God's ear to hear me,
God's word to speak to me,
God's hand to guard me,
God's way to lie before me,
God's shield to protect me,
God's host to save me,

From snares of devils,
From temptation of vices,
From every one who shall wish me ill,
Afar and anear,
Alone and in a multitude.

I summon today all these powers between me and
those evils,
Against every cruel, merciless power that may
oppose my body and soul,
Against incantations of false prophets,
Against black laws of pagandom,
Against false laws of heretics,
Against craft of idolatry,
Against spells of women, and smiths, and wizards,
Against every knowledge that corrupts man's body
and soul.

Christ to shield me today,
Against poisoning, against burning,
Against drowning, against wounding,
So there come to me abundance of reward.
Christ with me, Christ before me, Christ behind
me,
Christ in me, Christ beneath me, Christ above
me,
Christ on my right, Christ on my left,
Christ when I lie down, Christ when I sit down,
Christ when I arise,
Christ in the heart of every man who thinks of me,
Christ in the mouth of every one who speaks of me,
Christ in every eye that sees me,
Christ in every ear that hears me.

I arise today
Through a mighty strength, the invocation of the
    Trinity,
Through belief in the threeness,
Through confession of the oneness
Of the Creator of Creation.

[Translator: Kuno Meyer]

Biblical Reading: Daniel 5:31—6:1-23

Darius the Mede received the kingdom, being about sixty-two years old.

It pleased Darius to set over the kingdom one hundred twenty satraps, stationed throughout the whole kingdom, and over them three presidents, including Daniel; to these the satraps gave account so that the king might suffer no loss. Soon Daniel distinguished himself above all the other presidents and satraps because an excellent spirit was in him, and the king planned to appoint him over the whole kingdom. So the presidents and the satraps tried to find grounds for complaint against Daniel in connection with the kingdom. But they could find no grounds for complaint or any corruption, because he was faithful, and no negligence or corruption could be found in him. The men said, "We shall not find any ground for complaint against this Daniel unless we find it in connection with the law of his God."

So the presidents and satraps conspired and came to the king and said to him, "O King Darius, live forever! All the presidents of the kingdom, the prefects and the satraps, the counselors and the governors are agreed that the king should establish an ordinance and enforce an interdict, that whoever prays to anyone, divine or human, for thirty days, except to you, O king, shall be thrown into a den of lions. Now, O king, establish the interdict and sign the document, so that it cannot be changed, according to the law of the Medes and the Persians, which cannot be revoked." Therefore King Darius signed the document and the interdict.

Although Daniel knew that the document had been signed, he continued to go to his house, which had windows in its upper room opened toward Jerusalem, and to get down on his knees three times a day to pray to his God and praise him, just as he had done previously. The conspirators came and found Daniel praying and seeking mercy before his God. Then they approached the king and said concerning the interdict, "O king! Did you not sign an interdict, that anyone who prays to anyone, divine or human, within thirty days except to you, O king, shall be thrown into a den of lions?" The king answered, "the thing stands fast, according to the law of the Medes and Persians, which cannot be revoked." Then they responded to the king, "Daniel, one of the exiles from Judah, pays no attention to you, O king, or to the interdict you have signed, but he is saying his prayers three times a day."

When the king heard the charge, he was very much distressed. He was determined to save Daniel, and until the sun went down he made every effort to rescue him. Then the conspirators came to the king and said to him, "Know, O king, that it is a law of the Medes and Persians that no interdict or ordinance that the king establishes can be changed."

Then the king gave the command, and Daniel was brought and thrown into the den of lions. The king said to Daniel, "May your God, whom you faithfully serve, deliver you!" A stone was brought and laid on the mouth of the den, and the king sealed it with his own signet and with the signet of his lords, so that nothing might be changed concerning Daniel. Then the king went to his palace and spent the night fasting; no food was brought to him, and sleep fled from him.

Then, at break of day, the king got up and hurried to the den of lions. When he came near the den where Daniel was, he cried out anxiously to Daniel, "O Daniel, servant of the living God, has your God whom you faithfully serve been able to deliver you from the lions?" Daniel then said to the king: "O king, live forever! My God sent his angel and shut the lions' mouths so that they would not hurt me, because I was found blameless before him; and also before you, O king. I have done no wrong."

Novena Prayer

Our God, You are the God of all people.

You are the God of Heaven and earth, the God of the sea and the rivers, the God of the sun and the moon and all the stars, the God of the high mountains and the deep valleys.

O God, You are above the heavens, and in the heavens, and below the heavens.

You dwell in the heavens and on the earth, and in the sea, and in all the places therein.

You inspire all things, You give life to all things, You are above all things, You are below all things.

You give the sun its light,

You give the night and the stars their light,

You make springs of water in the desert and dry islands in the sea,

and You make the stars to serve the greater lights.

You have a Son Who is co-eternal with Yourself, and like Yourself in every way;

Your Son is no younger than You, O Father, nor are You, O Father, older than Your Son, and the Holy Spirit breathes through both the Father and the Son, and You, O God, are one, Father, Son, and Holy Spirit.

In the name of St. Patrick, Apostle of Ireland, I place my prayer before You and ask that, through his intercession You may grant my petition that *[name your petition here]* if it be according to Your will.

Day 4: The Three Young Men in the Furnace

Breastplate of St. Patrick

I arise today
Through a mighty strength, the invocation of the
    Trinity,
Through belief in the threeness,
Through confession of the oneness
Of the Creator of Creation.

I arise today
Through the strength of Christ's birth with His
    baptism,
Through the strength of His crucifixion with His
    burial,
Through the strength of His resurrection with His
    ascension,
Through the strength of His descent for the judg-
    ment of Doom.

I arise today
Through the strength of the love of the Cherubim,
In the obedience of angels,
In the service of archangels,
In the hope of the resurrection to meet with re-
    ward,
In the prayers of patriarchs,
In prediction of prophets,

In preaching of apostles,
In faith of confessors,
In innocence of holy virgins,
In deeds of righteous men.

I arise today
Through the strength of heaven,
Light of sun,
Radiance of moon,
Splendor of fire,
Speed of lightning,
Swiftness of wind,
Depth of sea,
Stability of earth,
Firmness of rock.

I arise today
Through God's strength to pilot me,
God's might to uphold me,
God's wisdom to guide me,
God's eye to look before me,
God's ear to hear me,
God's word to speak to me,
God's hand to guard me,
God's way to lie before me,
God's shield to protect me,
God's host to save me,
From snares of devils,
From temptation of vices,
From every one who shall wish me ill,
Afar and anear,
Alone and in a multitude.

I summon today all these powers between me and
   those evils,

Against every cruel, merciless power that may
    oppose my body and soul,
Against incantations of false prophets,
Against black laws of pagandom,
Against false laws of heretics,
Against craft of idolatry,
Against spells of women, and smiths, and wizards,
Against every knowledge that corrupts man's body
    and soul.

Christ to shield me today,
Against poisoning, against burning,
Against drowning, against wounding,
So there come to me abundance of reward.
Christ with me, Christ before me, Christ behind
    me,
Christ in me, Christ beneath me, Christ above me,
Christ on my right, Christ on my left,
Christ when I lie down, Christ when I sit down,
Christ when I arise,
Christ in the heart of every man who thinks of me,
Christ in the mouth of every one who speaks of me,
Christ in every eye that sees me,
Christ in every ear that hears me.

I arise today
Through a mighty strength, the invocation of the
    Trinity,
Through belief in the threeness,
Through confession of the oneness
Of the Creator of Creation.

[Translator: Kuno Meyer]

Biblical Reading: Daniel 3:1-13; 16-23; 91-97

King Nubuchadnezzar made a golden statue whose height was sixty cubits and whose width was six cubits; he set it up on the plain of Dura in the province of Babylon. Then King Nebuchadnezzar sent for the satraps, the prefects, and the governors, the counselors, the treasurers, the justices, the magistrates, and all the officials of the provinces to assemble and come to the dedication of the statue that King Nebuchadnezzar had set up. So the satraps, the prefects, and the governors, the counselors, the treasurers, the justices, the magistrates, and all the officials of the privinces assembled for the dedication of the statue that King Nebuchadnezzar had set up. When they were standing before the statue that Nebuchadnezzar had set up, the herald proclaimed aloud, "You are commanded O peoples, nations, and language, that when you hear the sound of the horn, pipe, lyre, trigon, harp, drum, and entire musical ensemble, you are to fall down and worship the golden statue that King Nebuchadnezzar has set up. Whoever does not fall down and worship shall immediately be thrown into a furnace of blazing fire." Therefore, as soon as all the peoples heard the sound of the horn, pipe, lyre, trigon, harp, drum, and entire musical ensemble, all the peoples, nations, and languages fell down and worshiped the golden statue that King Nebuchadnezzar had set up.

Accordingly, at this time certain Chaldeans came forward and denounced the Jews. They said to King Nebuchadnezzar, "O king, live forever! You, O king, have made a decree, that everyone who hears the sound of the horn, pipe, lyre, trigon, harp, drum, and entire musical ensemble, shall fall down and worship the golden statue, and whoever does not fall down and worship shall be thrown into a furnace of blazing fire. There are certain Jews whom you have appointed over the affairs of the province of Babylon: Shadrach, Meshach, and Abednego. These pay no heed to you, O King. They do not serve your gods and they do not worship the golden statue that you have set up."

Then Nebuchadnezzar in a furious rage commanded that Shadrach, Meshach, and Abednego be brought in; so they brought those men before the king.

Shadrach, Meshach, and Abednego answered the king, "O Nebuchadnezzar, we have no need to present a defense to you in this matter. If our God whom we serve is able to deliver us from the furnace of blazing fire and out of your hand, O king, let him deliver us! But if not, be it known to you, O king, that we will not serve your gods and we will not worship the golden statue you have set up."

Then Nebuchadnezzar was so filled with rage against Shadrach, Meshach, and Abednego that his face was distorted. He ordered the furnace heated up seven times more than was customary, and ordered some of the strongest guards in his army to bind Shadrach, Meshach, and Abednego and to throw them into the furnace of blazing fire. So the men were bound, still wearing their tunics, their trousers, their hats, and their other garments and they were thrown into the furnace of blazing fire. Because the king's command was urgent and the furnace was so overheated, the raging flames killed the men who lifted Shadrach, Meshach, and Abednego. But the three men, Shadrach, Meshach, and Abednego, fell down, bound, into the furnace of blazing fire.

Hearing them sing and amazed at seeing them alive, King Nebuchadnezzar rose up quickly. He said to his counselors, "Was it not three men that we threw bound into the fire?" They answered the king, "True, O king." He replied, "But I see four men unbound, walking in the middle of the fire, and they are not hurt; and the fourth has the appearance of a god." Nebuchadnezzar then approached the door of the furnace of blazing fire and said, "Shadrach, Meshach, and Abednego, servants of the Most High God, come out! Come here!" So Shadrach, Meshach, and Abednego came out from the fire. And the satraps, the prefects, the governors, and the king's counselors gathered together and saw that the fire had not had any power over the bodies of those men; the hair of their heads was not singed, their tunics were not harmed, and not even the smell of fire came from them. Nebuchadnezzar said: "Blessed be the God of Shadrach, Meshach, and Abednego, who has sent his angel and delivered his servants who trusted in him. They disobeyed the king's command and yielded up their bodies rather than worship any god except their own God. Therefore I make a decree: Any people, nation, or language that utters blasphemy against the God of Shadrach, Meshach, and Abednego shall be torn limb from limb, and their houses laid in ruins; for there is no other god who is able to deliver in this way." Then the king promoted Shadrach, Meshach, and Abednego in the province of Babylon.

Novena Prayer

Our God, You are the God of all people.

You are the God of Heaven and earth, the God of the sea and the rivers, the God of the sun and the moon and all the stars, the God of the high mountains and the deep valleys.

O God, You are above the heavens, and in the heavens, and below the heavens.

You dwell in the heavens and on the earth, and in the sea, and in all the places therein.

You inspire all things, You give life to all things, You are above all things, You are below all things.

You give the sun its light,

You give the night and the stars their light,

You make springs of water in the desert and dry islands in the sea,

and You make the stars to serve the greater lights.

You have a Son Who is co-eternal with Yourself, and like Yourself in every way;

Your Son is no younger than You, O Father, nor are You, O Father, older than Your Son, and the Holy Spirit breathes through both the Father and the Son, and You, O God, are one, Father, Son, and Holy Spirit.

In the name of St. Patrick, Apostle of Ireland, I place my prayer before You and ask that, through his intercession You may grant my petition that *[name your petition here]* if it be according to Your will.

Day 5: The Flight into Egypt

Breastplate of St. Patrick

I arise today
Through a mighty strength, the invocation of the
    Trinity,
Through belief in the threeness,
Through confession of the oneness
Of the Creator of Creation.

I arise today
Through the strength of Christ's birth with His
    baptism,
Through the strength of His crucifixion with His
    burial,
Through the strength of His resurrection with His
    ascension,
Through the strength of His descent for the judg-
    ment of Doom.

I arise today
Through the strength of the love of the Cherubim,
In the obedience of angels,
In the service of archangels,
In the hope of the resurrection to meet with re-
    ward,
In the prayers of patriarchs,
In prediction of prophets,

In preaching of apostles,
In faith of confessors,
In innocence of holy virgins,
In deeds of righteous men.

I arise today
Through the strength of heaven,
Light of sun,
Radiance of moon,
Splendor of fire,
Speed of lightning,
Swiftness of wind,
Depth of sea,
Stability of earth,
Firmness of rock.

I arise today
Through God's strength to pilot me,
God's might to uphold me,
God's wisdom to guide me,
God's eye to look before me,
God's ear to hear me,
God's word to speak to me,
God's hand to guard me,
God's way to lie before me,
God's shield to protect me,
God's host to save me,
From snares of devils,
From temptation of vices,
From every one who shall wish me ill,
Afar and anear,
Alone and in a multitude.

I summon today all these powers between me and
    those evils,

Against every cruel, merciless power that may
 oppose my body and soul,
Against incantations of false prophets,
Against black laws of pagandom,
Against false laws of heretics,
Against craft of idolatry,
Against spells of women, and smiths, and wizards,
Against every knowledge that corrupts man's body
 and soul.

Christ to shield me today,
Against poisoning, against burning,
Against drowning, against wounding,
So there come to me abundance of reward.
Christ with me, Christ before me, Christ behind
 me,
Christ in me, Christ beneath me, Christ above me,
Christ on my right, Christ on my left,
Christ when I lie down, Christ when I sit down,
Christ when I arise,
Christ in the heart of every man who thinks of me,
Christ in the mouth of every one who speaks of me,
Christ in every eye that sees me,
Christ in every ear that hears me.

I arise today
Through a mighty strength, the invocation of the
 Trinity,
Through belief in the threeness,
Through confession of the oneness
Of the Creator of Creation.

[Translator: Kuno Meyer]

Biblical Reading: Matthew 2:13-15

Now after they had left, an angel of the Lord appeared to Joseph in a dream and said, "Get up, take the child and his mother, and flee to Egypt, and remain there until I tell you; for Herod is about to search for the child, to destroy him." Then Joseph got up, took the child and his mother by night, and went to Egypt, and remained there until the death of Herod. This was to fulfill what had been spoken by the Lord through the prophet: *"Out of Egypt, I have called my son."*

Novena Prayer

Our God, You are the God of all people.

You are the God of Heaven and earth, the God of the sea and the rivers, the God of the sun and the moon and all the stars, the God of the high mountains and the deep valleys.

O God, You are above the heavens, and in the heavens, and below the heavens.

You dwell in the heavens and on the earth, and in the sea, and in all the places therein.

You inspire all things, You give life to all things, You are above all things, You are below all things.

You give the sun its light,

You give the night and the stars their light,

You make springs of water in the desert and dry islands in the sea,

and You make the stars to serve the greater lights.

You have a Son Who is co-eternal with Yourself, and like Yourself in every way;

Your Son is no younger than You, O Father, nor are You, O Father, older than Your Son, and the Holy Spirit breathes through both the Father and the Son, and You, O God, are one, Father, Son, and Holy Spirit.

In the name of St. Patrick, Apostle of Ireland, I place my prayer before You and ask that, through his intercession You may grant my petition that *[name your petition here]* if it be according to Your will.

Day 6: The Twelve Apostles

Breastplate of St. Patrick

I arise today
Through a mighty strength, the invocation of the
   Trinity,
Through belief in the threeness,
Through confession of the oneness
Of the Creator of Creation.

I arise today
Through the strength of Christ's birth with His
   baptism,
Through the strength of His crucifixion with His
   burial,
Through the strength of His resurrection with His
   ascension,
Through the strength of His descent for the judgment of Doom.

I arise today
Through the strength of the love of the Cherubim,
In the obedience of angels,
In the service of archangels,
In the hope of the resurrection to meet with reward,
In the prayers of patriarchs,
In prediction of prophets,
In preaching of apostles,
In faith of confessors,
In innocence of holy virgins,
In deeds of righteous men.

I arise today
Through the strength of heaven,
Light of sun,
Radiance of moon,
Splendor of fire,
Speed of lightning,
Swiftness of wind,
Depth of sea,
Stability of earth,
Firmness of rock.

I arise today
Through God's strength to pilot me,
God's might to uphold me,
God's wisdom to guide me,
God's eye to look before me,
God's ear to hear me,
God's word to speak to me,
God's hand to guard me,
God's way to lie before me,
God's shield to protect me,
God's host to save me,

From snares of devils,
From temptation of vices,
From every one who shall wish me ill,
Afar and anear,
Alone and in a multitude.

I summon today all these powers between me and
    those evils,
Against every cruel, merciless power that may
    oppose my body and soul,
Against incantations of false prophets,
Against black laws of pagandom,
Against false laws of heretics,
Against craft of idolatry,
Against spells of women, and smiths, and wizards,
Against every knowledge that corrupts man's body
    and soul.

Christ to shield me today,
Against poisoning, against burning,
Against drowning, against wounding,
So there come to me abundance of reward.
Christ with me, Christ before me, Christ behind
    me,
Christ in me, Christ beneath me, Christ above me,
Christ on my right, Christ on my left,
Christ when I lie down, Christ when I sit down,
Christ when I arise,
Christ in the heart of every man who thinks of me,
Christ in the mouth of every one who speaks of me,
Christ in every eye that sees me,
Christ in every ear that hears me.

I arise today
Through a mighty strength, the invocation of the
    Trinity,

Through belief in the threeness,
Through confession of the oneness
Of the Creator of Creation.

[Translator: Kuno Meyer]

Biblical Reading: Matthew 10:1-13

Then Jesus summoned his twelve disciples and gave them authority over unclean spirits, to cast them out, and to cure every disease and every sickness. These are the names of the twelve apostles: first, Simon, also known as Peter, and his brother Andrew; James son of Zebedee, and his brother John; Philip and Bartholomew; Thomas and Matthew the tax collector; James son of Alphaeus, and Thaddeus; Simon the Cananean, and Judas Iscariot, the one who betrayed him.

These twelve Jesus sent out with the following instructions: "Go nowhere among the Gentiles, and enter no town of the Samaritans, but go rather to the lost sheep of the house of Israel. As you go, proclaim the good news, 'The kingdom of heaven has come near.' Cure the sick, raise the dead, cleanse the lepers, cast out demons. You received without payment; give without payment. Take no gold, or silver, or copper in your belts, no bag for your journey, or two tunics, or sandals, or a staff; for the laborers deserve their food. Whatever town or village you enter, find out who in it is worthy, and stay there until you leave. As you enter the house, greet it. If the house is worthy, let your peace come upon it; but if it is not worthy, let your peace return to you.

Novena Prayer

Our God, You are the God of all people.

You are the God of Heaven and earth, the God of the sea and the rivers, the God of the sun and the moon and all the stars, the God of the high mountains and the deep valleys.

O God, You are above the heavens, and in the heavens, and below the heavens.

You dwell in the heavens and on the earth, and in the sea, and in all the places therein.

You inspire all things, You give life to all things, You are above all things, You are below all things.

You give the sun its light,

You give the night and the stars their light,

You make springs of water in the desert and dry islands in the sea,

and You make the stars to serve the greater lights.

You have a Son Who is co-eternal with Yourself, and like Yourself in every way;

Your Son is no younger than You, O Father, nor are You, O Father, older than Your Son, and the Holy Spirit breathes through both the Father and the Son, and You, O God, are one, Father, Son, and Holy Spirit.

In the name of St. Patrick, Apostle of Ireland, I place my prayer before You and ask that, through his intercession You may grant my petition that *[name your petition here]* if it be according to Your will.

Day 7: The Loaves and the Fishes

Breastplate of St. Patrick

I arise today
Through a mighty strength, the invocation of the
    Trinity,
Through belief in the threeness,
Through confession of the oneness
Of the Creator of Creation.

I arise today
Through the strength of Christ's birth with His
    baptism,
Through the strength of His crucifixion with His
    burial,
Through the strength of His resurrection with His
    ascension,
Through the strength of His descent for the judg-
    ment of Doom.

I arise today
Through the strength of the love of the Cherubim,
In the obedience of angels,
In the service of archangels,
In the hope of the resurrection to meet with re-
    ward,
In the prayers of patriarchs,
In prediction of prophets,

In preaching of apostles,
In faith of confessors,
In innocence of holy virgins,
In deeds of righteous men.

I arise today
Through the strength of heaven,
Light of sun,
Radiance of moon,
Splendor of fire,
Speed of lightning,
Swiftness of wind,
Depth of sea,
Stability of earth,
Firmness of rock.

I arise today
Through God's strength to pilot me,
God's might to uphold me,
God's wisdom to guide me,
God's eye to look before me,
God's ear to hear me,
God's word to speak to me,
God's hand to guard me,
God's way to lie before me,
God's shield to protect me,
God's host to save me,
From snares of devils,
From temptation of vices,
From every one who shall wish me ill,
Afar and anear,
Alone and in a multitude.

I summon today all these powers between me and
those evils,

Against every cruel, merciless power that may
oppose my body and soul,
Against incantations of false prophets,
Against black laws of pagandom,
Against false laws of heretics,
Against craft of idolatry,
Against spells of women, and smiths, and wizards,
Against every knowledge that corrupts man's body
and soul.

Christ to shield me today,
Against poisoning, against burning,
Against drowning, against wounding,
So there come to me abundance of reward.
Christ with me, Christ before me, Christ behind
me,
Christ in me, Christ beneath me, Christ above me,
Christ on my right, Christ on my left,
Christ when I lie down, Christ when I sit down,
Christ when I arise,
Christ in the heart of every man who thinks of me,
Christ in the mouth of every one who speaks of me,
Christ in every eye that sees me,
Christ in every ear that hears me.

I arise today
Through a mighty strength, the invocation of the
Trinity,
Through belief in the threeness,
Through confession of the oneness
Of the Creator of Creation.

[Translator: Kuno Meyer]

Biblical Reading: Matthew 14:14-21

When he went ashore, he saw a great crowd; and he had compassion for them and cured their sick. When it was evening, the disciples came to him and said, "This is a deserted place, and the hour is now late; send the crowds away so that they may go into the villages and buy food for themselves." Jesus said to them, "They need not go away; you give them something to eat." They replied, "We have nothing here but five loaves and two fish." And he said, "Bring them here to me." Then he ordered the crowds to sit down on the grass. Taking the five loaves and two fish, he looked up to heaven, and blessed and broke the loaves, and gave them to the disciples, and the disciples gave them to the crowds. And all ate and were filled; and they took up what was left over of the broken pieces, twelve baskets full. And those who ate were about five thousand men, besides women and children.

Novena Prayer

Our God, You are the God of all people.

You are the God of Heaven and earth, the God of the sea and the rivers, the God of the sun and the moon and all the stars, the God of the high mountains and the deep valleys.

O God, You are above the heavens, and in the heavens, and below the heavens.

You dwell in the heavens and on the earth, and in the sea, and in all the places therein.

You inspire all things, You give life to all things, You are above all things, You are below all things.

You give the sun its light,
You give the night and the stars their light,
You make springs of water in the desert and dry
  islands in the sea,
and You make the stars to serve the greater lights.
You have a Son Who is co-eternal with Yourself,
  and like Yourself in every way;
Your Son is no younger than You, O Father, nor
  are You, O Father, older than Your Son, and the
  Holy Spirit breathes through both the Father
  and the Son, and You, O God, are one, Father,
  Son, and Holy Spirit.
In the name of St. Patrick, Apostle of Ireland, I
  place my prayer before You and ask that,
  through his intercession You may grant my petition that *[name your petition here]* if it be according to Your will.

Day 8: The Crucifixion
Breastplate of St. Patrick

I arise today
Through a mighty strength, the invocation of the
  Trinity,
Through belief in the threeness,
Through confession of the oneness

Of the Creator of Creation.

I arise today
Through the strength of Christ's birth with His
   baptism,
Through the strength of His crucifixion with His
   burial,
Through the strength of His resurrection with His
   ascension,
Through the strength of His descent for the judgment of Doom.

I arise today
Through the strength of the love of the Cherubim,
In the obedience of angels,
In the service of archangels,
In the hope of the resurrection to meet with re-
   ward,
In the prayers of patriarchs,
In prediction of prophets,
In preaching of apostles,
In faith of confessors,
In innocence of holy virgins,
In deeds of righteous men.

I arise today
Through the strength of heaven,
Light of sun,
Radiance of moon,
Splendor of fire,
Speed of lightning,
Swiftness of wind,
Depth of sea,
Stability of earth,
Firmness of rock.

I arise today
Through God's strength to pilot me,
God's might to uphold me,
God's wisdom to guide me,
God's eye to look before me,
God's ear to hear me,
God's word to speak to me,
God's hand to guard me,
God's way to lie before me,
God's shield to protect me,
God's host to save me,
From snares of devils,
From temptation of vices,
From every one who shall wish me ill,
Afar and anear,
Alone and in a multitude.

I summon today all these powers between me and
    those evils,
Against every cruel, merciless power that may
    oppose my body and soul,
Against incantations of false prophets,
Against black laws of pagandom,
Against false laws of heretics,
Against craft of idolatry,
Against spells of women, and smiths, and wizards,
Against every knowledge that corrupts man's body
    and soul.

Christ to shield me today,
Against poisoning, against burning,
Against drowning, against wounding,
So there come to me abundance of reward.
Christ with me, Christ before me, Christ behind
    me,

Christ in me, Christ beneath me, Christ above me,
Christ on my right, Christ on my left,
Christ when I lie down, Christ when I sit down,
Christ when I arise,
Christ in the heart of every man who thinks of me,
Christ in the mouth of every one who speaks of me,
Christ in every eye that sees me,
Christ in every ear that hears me.

I arise today
Through a mighty strength, the invocation of the
 Trinity,
Through belief in the threeness,
Through confession of the oneness
Of the Creator of Creation.

[Translator: Kuno Meyer]

Biblical Reading: Mark 15:24-39

And they crucified him, and *divided* his *clothes* among them, *casting lots* to decide what each should take.

It was nine o'clock in the morning when they crucified him. The inscription of the charge against him read, "The King of the Jews." And with him they crucified two bandits, one on his right and the one on his left. Those who passed by derided him, *shaking* their *heads* and saying, "Aha! You who would destroy the temple and build it in three days, save yourself and come down from the cross!" In the same way the chief priests, along with the scribes, were also mocking him among themselves and saying, "He saved others; he cannot save himself. Let the Messiah, the King of

Israel, come down from the cross now, so that we may see and believe." Those who were crucified with him also taunted him.

When it was noon, darkness came over the whole land until three in the afternoon. At three o'clock Jesus cried out with a loud voice, *"Eloi, Eloi, lema sabachthani?"* which means, *"My God, my God, why have you forsaken me?"* When some of the bystanders heard it, they said, "Listen, he is calling for Elijah." And someone ran, filled a sponge with *sour wine,* put it on a stick, and *gave it* to him *to drink,* saying, "Wait, let us see whether Elijah will come to take him down." Then Jesus gave a loud cry and breathed his last. And the curtain of the temple was torn in two, from top to bottom. Now when the centurion, who stood facing him, saw that in this way he breathed his last, he said, "Truly this man was God's Son."

Novena Prayer

Our God, You are the God of all people.

You are the God of Heaven and earth, the God of the sea and the rivers, the God of the sun and the moon and all the stars, the God of the high mountains and the deep valleys.

O God, You are above the heavens, and in the heavens, and below the heavens.

You dwell in the heavens and on the earth, and in the sea, and in all the places therein.

You inspire all things, You give life to all things, You are above all things, You are below all things.

You give the sun its light,

You give the night and the stars their light,

You make springs of water in the desert and dry islands in the sea,

and You make the stars to serve the greater lights.

You have a Son Who is co-eternal with Yourself, and like Yourself in every way;

Your Son is no younger than You, O Father, nor are You, O Father, older than Your Son, and the Holy Spirit breathes through both the Father and the Son, and You, O God, are one, Father, Son, and Holy Spirit.

In the name of St. Patrick, Apostle of Ireland, I place my prayer before You and ask that, through his intercession You may grant my petition that *[name your petition here]* if it be according to Your will.

Day 9: The Crucifixion

Breastplate of St. Patrick

I arise today

Through a mighty strength, the invocation of the Trinity,

Through belief in the threeness,

Through confession of the oneness
Of the Creator of Creation.

I arise today
Through the strength of Christ's birth with His
   baptism,
Through the strength of His crucifixion with His
   burial,
Through the strength of His resurrection with His
   ascension,
Through the strength of His descent for the judgment of Doom.

I arise today
Through the strength of the love of the Cherubim,
In the obedience of angels,
In the service of archangels,
In the hope of the resurrection to meet with re-
   ward,
In the prayers of patriarchs,
In prediction of prophets,
In preaching of apostles,
In faith of confessors,
In innocence of holy virgins,
In deeds of righteous men.

I arise today
Through the strength of heaven,
Light of sun,
Radiance of moon,
Splendor of fire,
Speed of lightning,
Swiftness of wind,
Depth of sea,
Stability of earth,
Firmness of rock.

I arise today
Through God's strength to pilot me,
God's might to uphold me,
God's wisdom to guide me,
God's eye to look before me,
God's ear to hear me,
God's word to speak to me,
God's hand to guard me,
God's way to lie before me,
God's shield to protect me,
God's host to save me,
From snares of devils,
From temptation of vices,
From every one who shall wish me ill,
Afar and anear,
Alone and in a multitude.

I summon today all these powers between me and
  those evils,
Against every cruel, merciless power that may
  oppose my body and soul,
Against incantations of false prophets,
Against black laws of pagandom,
Against false laws of heretics,
Against craft of idolatry,
Against spells of women, and smiths, and wizards,
Against every knowledge that corrupts man's body
  and soul.

Christ to shield me today,
Against poisoning, against burning,
Against drowning, against wounding,
So there come to me abundance of reward.
Christ with me, Christ before me, Christ behind
  me,

Christ in me, Christ beneath me, Christ above me,
Christ on my right, Christ on my left,
Christ when I lie down, Christ when I sit down,
Christ when I arise,
Christ in the heart of every man who thinks of me,
Christ in the mouth of every one who speaks of me,
Christ in every eye that sees me,
Christ in every ear that hears me.

I arise today
Through a mighty strength, the invocation of the
    Trinity,
Through belief in the threeness,
Through confession of the oneness
Of the Creator of Creation.

[Translator: Kuno Meyer]

Biblical Reading: John 19:17-30

And, carrying the cross, by himself, he went out to what is called The Place of the Skull, which in Hebrew is called Golgotha. There they crucified him, and with him two others, one on either side, with Jesus between them. Pilate also had an inscription written and put on the cross. It read, "Jesus of Nazareth, the King of the Jews." Many of the Jews read this inscription, because the place where Jesus was crucified was near the city; and it was written in Hebrew, in Latin, and in Greek. Then the chief priests of the Jews said to Pilate, "Do not write, 'The King of the Jews,' but, 'This man said, I am the King of the Jews.' " Pilate answered, "What I have written I have written." When the soldiers had crucified Jesus, they took his clothes and divided them into four parts, one for each soldier. They also took his tunic; now the tunic was seamless, woven in one piece from the top. So they said to one another, "Let us not tear it, but cast lots for it to see who will get it." This was to fulfill what the scripture says,

> "They divided my clothes among themselves,
>   and for my clothing they cast lots."

And that is what the soldiers did.

Meanwhile, standing near the cross of Jesus were his mother, and his mother's sister, Mary the wife of Clopas, and Mary Magdalene. When Jesus saw his mother and the disciple whom he loved standing beside her, he said to his mother, "Woman, here is your son." Then he said to the disciple, "Here is your mother." And from that hour the disciple took her into his home.

After this, when Jesus knew that all was now finished, he said (in order to fulfill the scripture), "I am thirsty." A jar full of sour wine was standing there. So they put a sponge full of the wine on a branch of hyssop and held it to his mouth. When Jesus had received the wine, he said, "It is finished." Then he bowed his head and gave up his spirit.

Novena Prayer

Our God, You are the God of all people.

You are the God of Heaven and earth, the God of the sea and the rivers, the God of the sun and the moon and all the stars, the God of the high mountains and the deep valleys.

O God, You are above the heavens, and in the heavens, and below the heavens.

You dwell in the heavens and on the earth, and in the sea, and in all the places therein.

You inspire all things, You give life to all things, You are above all things, You are below all things.

You give the sun its light,

You give the night and the stars their light,

You make springs of water in the desert and dry islands in the sea,

and You make the stars to serve the greater lights.

You have a Son Who is co-eternal with Yourself, and like Yourself in every way;

Your Son is no younger than You, O Father, nor are You, O Father, older than Your Son, and the Holy Spirit breathes through both the Father and the Son, and You, O God, are one, Father, Son, and Holy Spirit.

In the name of St. Patrick, Apostle of Ireland, I place my prayer before You and ask that, through his intercession You may grant my petition that *[name your petition here]* if it be according to Your will.

– 6 –

Official Mass of St. Patrick

**Courtesy of the National Centre for Liturgy,
St Patrick's College, Maynooth, Co. Kildare, Ireland.**

Although St. Patrick's Day is only a commemoration in the General Roman Calendar and the editio typica of the Roman Missal just gives a Collect for the Mass, in Ireland this feast day is a solemnity. The Irish Episcopal Conference composed a full Mass for this day. The official texts of this Mass and the references to its Scripture readings are provided below. Although these texts are officially approved for use only in Ireland (and are not licit for liturgical use elsewhere), nonetheless the Church recognizes that all official prayer texts are a valid aid to personal prayer (see Catechism of the Catholic Church, 1124). It is hoped that by providing them here they might serve as an additional source of prayer.

March 17

**Saint Patrick, Bishop
Principal Patron of Ireland**

Solemnity

Entrance Antiphon Gen 12:1-2

Go from your country and your kindred and your father's house to the land that I will show you. I will make of you a great nation, and I will

135

bless you, and make your name great, so that you will be a blessing.

Collect

Lord , through the work of Saint Patrick in Ireland
we have come to acknowledge the mystery of the
  one true God
and give thanks for our salvation in Christ;
grant by his prayers
that we who celebrate this festival
may keep alive the fire of faith he kindled.
Through our Lord Jesus Christ, your Son,
who lives and reigns with you and the Holy Spirit,
one God, for ever and ever.

Readings: Year A

First Reading: Sirach (Eccles) 39:6-10

His memory will not disappear and his name will live through all generations.

Responsorial Psalm: Psalm 115:12-19. R/. v. 12

Second Reading: 2 Timothy 4:1-8

Convince, rebuke and encourage, with the utmost patience in teaching.

Gospel Acclamation: James 1:21

Glory to you, O Christ, you are the Word of God!
Accept and submit to the word which has been
  planted in you and can save your souls.
Glory to you, O Christ, you are the Word of God!

Gospel Reading: Matthew 13:24-32

It is the smallest of all the seeds, but when it has grown it is the greatest of shrubs.

Readings: Year B

First Reading: Jeremiah 1:4-9

You shall go to all to whom I send you.

Responsorial Psalm: Psalm 116. R/. Mark 16:15

Response: Go out to the whole world: proclaim the Good News.

Second Reading: Romans 10:9-18

Faith comes from what is heard, through the Word of Christ.

Gospel Acclamation: Matthew 28:19-20

Glory to you, O Christ, you are the Word of God!
Go, make disciples of all nations, says the Lord; I am
  with you always, yes, to the end of time.
Glory to you, O Christ, you are the Word of God!

Gospel Reading: Mark 16:15-20

They went out and proclaimed the good news everywhere.

Readings: Year C

First Reading: Amos 7:12-15

The Lord took me from following the flock.

Responsorial Psalm: Psalm 138:1-3, 7-10, 13-14. R/v. 9-10

Second Reading: 1 Thessalonians 2:2-8

We never came with words of flattery or with a pretext for greed.

Gospel Acclamation: Luke 4:18

Glory to you, O Christ, you are the Word of God!
The Lord has sent me to bring good news to the
poor, to proclaim liberty to captives.
Glory to you, O Christ, you are the Word of God!

Gospel Reading: Luke 5:1-11

"Lord, I am a sinful man." Jesus said, "Do not be afraid."

Prayer over the Gifts

Lord, accept this pure sacrifice
which, through the labors of Saint Patrick,
your grateful people make
to the glory of your name.
Through Jesus Christ our Lord.

Preface

℣. The Lord be with you.

℟. And also with you.

℣. Lift up your hearts.

℟. We lift them up to the Lord.

℣. Let us give thanks to the Lord our God.

℟. It is right to give him thanks and praise.

It is truly right and just, our duty and our salvation,
always and everywhere to give you thanks,
Lord, holy Father, almighty and eternal God,
and to offer you fitting praise
as we honor Saint Patrick.

For you drew him through daily prayer
in captivity and hardship

to know you as a loving Father.

You chose him out of all the world
to return to the land of his captors,
that they might acknowledge Jesus Christ, their
     Redeemer.

In the power of your Spirit you directed his paths
to win the sons and daughters of the Irish
to the service of the Triune God.

With joyful hearts we echo on earth
the song of the angels in heaven
as they praise your glory without end:

Holy, Holy, Holy…

Communion Antiphon Cf Mt 8:11

Many will come from east and west
and sit down with Abraham, Isaac and Jacob
at the feast in the kingdom of heaven, says the Lord.

Prayer after Communion
Strengthen us, O Lord, by this sacrament
so that we may profess the faith taught by Saint
     Patrick
and proclaim it in our way of living.
Through Christ our Lord.

Solemn Blessing
May God the Father, who called us together
to celebrate the feast of Saint Patrick,

bless you, protect you, and keep you faithful.

℟. Amen.

May Christ the Lord, the High King of Heaven,
be near you at all times.

℟. Amen

May the Holy Spirit, who is the source of all holi-
ness,
make you rich in the love of God's people.

℟. Amen

And may the blessing of almighty God,
the Father, and the Son, ✠ and the Holy Spirit
come down on you and remain for ever.

℟. Amen.

– 7 –

Further Reading

Many books have been written on St. Patrick and early Ireland. The following are recommended as starting points for those who are interested in delving more deeply into the life and world of the Saint.

Scholarly Editions of St. Patrick's Works

Ludwig Bieler. *The Works of St. Patrick, St. Secundinus and the Hymn on St. Patrick.* Mahwah, NJ: Paulist Press, 1953.

Professor Bieler has produced a very nice edition of the works of St. Patrick with comprehensive notes and introductions.

David R. Howlett. *The Book of Letters of Saint Patrick the Bishop.* Dublin: Four Courts Press, 1994.

This is an important textual study of St. Patrick's works. Although perhaps a little heavy for the general reader, for those who are up to the challenge Howlett provides very rewarding textual analysis of the Saint's writings.

St. Patrick's World

Liam de Paor. *Saint Patrick's World: The Christian Culture of Ireland's Apostolic Age.* Dublin: Four Courts Press, 1996.

This book provides English translations of many contemporary documents relating to St. Patrick's world and then of material relating to the early history of the Church in Ireland.

Regine Pernoud. *Martin of Tours: Soldier, Bishop, Saint.* San Francisco, CA: Ignatius Press, 2006.

While not specifically about St. Patrick or Ireland this beautiful little book about one of the greatest Saints of Late Antiquity provides a glimpse into the world St. Patrick inhabited, particularly given his own reference to his contacts with the Church in Gaul (see *Confessions* 43).

Peter Brown. *The Rise of Western Christendom.* Second Edition. Malden, MA: Blackwell Publishing, 2003.

A more scholarly (yet still very readable) introduction to the world of Late Antiquity and Western Europe in general at the time of St. Patrick is provided by Peter Brown, an expert in the field.

Introduction to the History of Ireland

Thomas M. Charles-Edwards. *Early Christian Ireland.* Cambridge: Cambridge University Press, 2000.

This book provides an academic treatment of the early development of the Church in Ireland in the period after St. Patrick.

Dáibhí Ó Cróinín. *A New History of Ireland, Vol. I: Prehistoric and Early Ireland.* Oxford: Oxford University Press, 2005.

Although some of the entries are actually quite dated, this book provides many essays on Irish history both before and after the introduction of Christianity in Ireland.

T.W. Moody and F.X. Martin, eds. *The Course of Irish History.* Fourth Edition. Lanham, MD: Roberts Rinehart Publishers, 2001.

This is the classic introduction to the history of Ireland covering all of her history from the prehistoric period all the way to the contemporary situation.

OTHER OUTSTANDING CATHOLIC BOOKS

AUGUSTINE ON PRAYER—An excellent summary of the great African Bishop's teaching on prayer in the life of Christians. Over 500 Augustinian texts. **Ask for No. 171**

SAINT AUGUSTINE: Man, Pastor, Mystic—By Rev. Augustine Trapé, O.S.A. A masterful biography of one of the greatest Saints in the Church by a world-renowned scholar. Large type and magnificently illustrated. **Ask for No. 172**

CONFESSIONS OF ST. AUGUSTINE—New translation of the Christian classic that –after the Bible and the Imitation of Christ—is the most widely translated and the most universally esteemed. It is published in prayerbook format as befits its nature.. **Ask for No. 173**

WORDS OF COMFORT FOR EVERY DAY—Short meditation for every day including a Scripture text and a meditative prayer to God the Father. Printed in two colors. 192 pages. **Ask for No. 186**

MARY DAY BY DAY—Minute meditations for every day of the year, including a Scripture passage, a quotation from the Saints, and a concluding prayer. Printed in two colors with over 300 illustrations. **Ask for No. 180**

MINUTE MEDITATIONS FROM THE POPES—By Rev. Jude Winkler, O.F.M. Conv. Minute meditations for every day of the year using the words of twentieth-century Popes. Printed and illustrated in two colors. **Ask for No. 175**

BIBLE DAY BY DAY—By Rev. John Kersten, S.V.D. Minute Bible meditations for every day including a short Scripture text and brief reflection. Printed in two colors with 300 illustrations. **Ask for No. 150**

LIVING WISDOM FOR EVERY DAY—By Rev. Bennet Kelley, C.P. Choice texts from St. Paul of the Cross, one of the true Masters of Spirituality, and a prayer for each day. **Ask for No. 182**

MINUTE MEDITATIONS FOR EACH DAY— By Rev. Bede Naegele O.C.D. This very attractive book offers a short Scripture text, a practical reflection, and a meaningful prayer for each day of the year. **Ask for No. 190**

WHEREVER CATHOLIC BOOKS ARE SOLD